the Difference
a Day Makes

the Difference a Day Makes

365 Ways to Change Your World in Just 24 Hours

KAREN M. JONES

New World Library
Novato, California

New World Library
14 Pamaron Way
Novato, California 94949

The material in this book is intended for education. Mention of an organization or Website should not be construed as an endorsement of its mission and/or content by the author or publisher.

Cover design by Mary Ann Casler
Author photograph by Guy Abernathey
Text design and typography by Tona Pearce Myers

Library of Congress Cataloging-in-Publication Data
Jones, Karen M.
  The difference a day makes : 365 ways to change your world in just 24 hours / Karen M. Jones.
      p.   cm.
  ISBN 1-57731-475-1 (pbk. : alk. paper)
  1. Social change. 2. Social action. 3. Community organization. I. Title.
  HM831.J66 2005
  303.4—dc22   2004019680

New World Library is dedicated to preserving the earth and its resources. We are now printing 50% of our new titles on 100% chlorine-free postconsumer waste recycled paper. As members of the Green Press Initiative (www.recycledproducts.org/gpi/), our goal is to use 100% recycled paper for all of our titles by 2007.

♺ Printed in Canada on 100% postconsumer waste recycled paper

First printing, January 2005
ISBN 1-57731-475-1
Distributed by Publishers Group West

10 9 8 7 6 5 4 3 2

For my mother, Jennie Marie McDermitt Jones,
who has made the difference in all of my days.

Contents

Introduction

It is not enough to be compassionate;
you must act.

— The Dalai Lama

In the winter of 2002, I was feeling permanently bruised by a series of traumatic national events. The shootings at Columbine High School, the murder of Matthew Shepard in Wyoming, the dragging of James Byrd behind a pickup truck until he died, and, finally, the September 11 attack on the World Trade Center first devastated me, then kindled a new and powerful resolve. I went looking for a way to help — to restore my faith in human kindness. But every volunteer coordinator wanted more time than I had available; every charity wanted a check that my bank balance wouldn't support; and every Web search overwhelmed me with more data and decisions than

I could process. I was sure that doing something good didn't have to be so difficult.

I began to research and compile the simple actions in this book for every well-intentioned person who'd rather make an effort than write a check but who simply can't find room in a hectic week for a sustained volunteer commitment. Each suggested action, in sixteen "helping" categories, can be started and finished in the course of a single day — some in five minutes — and none requires a cash donation. You can outfit a homeless person for a job interview, fund hunger relief (at no cost to you) with the click of a mouse, and help a troubled child earn awards in the arts. With "365 Ways to Change Your World in Just 24 Hours," you can set a goal of accomplishing a different step each day of the year. You can also activate the same tool, such as a click donation, every day. Or you can choose an issue that inspires the "everyday altruist" in you and take the actions in the relevant chapter as time permits.

"The Difference a Day Makes" turns the conventional model of volunteering — a few advocates doing enormous amounts of work — on its ear. It prescribes small change on a mass scale, which can be equally powerful. The book is not intended as a guide for fervent activism, but rather as a daily practice for personal and even spiritual growth through small, empowering acts of humanity. The causes themselves may be less important than your decision to overcome inertia and take a purposeful step. In addition to your personal use, this book may be used by community groups to implement service projects, by schools to engage students in compassionate action, by nonprofit groups as a thank-you to donors, and by businesses to boost employee morale with lively incentives for service. Its potential to create a chain of benevolence around the world is yours to launch.

Don't get me wrong; our world needs the check-writers and the formal volunteers who devote hours every day, week, or month to keep charitable efforts thriving. This book is for the considerable numbers of others who can help in other ways, if only you know where to start. With these first steps, you may discover a passion for a particular issue that makes you want to do more. Doing for others brings a joyous rush. You can't help but feel good once you start expressing your humanity — a phenomenon I call "philantherapy." We've spent decades consuming self-help, when perhaps self*less* help is the key to fulfillment and inner peace.

In time, practicing simple, everyday altruism gives you a glimpse of the grander notion that you can enrich your inner life by looking outward. We can all reconnect with our best intentions, tune in to our shared humanity, and reclaim our influence in a society that has convinced us, for too long, that individuals are insignificant. And we can do it without examining our navels, quitting our jobs, or running off to a religious retreat. We can do it, in fact, in just a few minutes a day.

You can start right away. Every day for a week, take the simple actions that resonate with you. Notice how it feels to demonstrate kindness routinely. Reclaim your influence and your vital role in a world you can change. You'll discover that the difference a day makes, while significant for recipients, is greatest for the giver.

You are also invited to join the online community of Benevolent Planet, where you'll find additional resources for everyday altruism; visit **benevolentplanet.com.**

A Word about Websites

Because the Internet has made a wealth of information, activity channels, and products available at the click of a mouse — making action steps easier and faster than ever — useful Websites are recommended throughout this book. While Websites and their addresses (URLs, or Universal Resource Locators) were live and current at the time of publication, Internet material is dynamic and may move or, occasionally, disappear altogether. For this reason, suggested keyword searches are provided to help you locate the recommended (or similar) material, and traditional contact information is given as an alternative avenue. You can also find a list of updated URLs

related to those in this book at **benevolentplanet.com;**
click on "The Difference a Day Makes."

Organizations' mailing addresses are also provided
for those without Internet access, and for those who simply prefer to make requests via postal mail. Please note
that some organizations must cover their mailing costs by
charging a nominal fee for information they send you
this way. Others with similar cost concerns may not
make Website information available in printed form.

Where URLs are provided, the standard "http://www"
portion has been omitted. To ensure access to a page, you
should reinstate this portion when entering a URL into
your browser.

Those without home Internet access may go online at
local libraries or Internet cafés; you may also ask a friend
or family member with Internet access to print out material for you.

the Difference
a Day Makes

CHAPTER ONE

Nature Nurture

Fill what's empty. Empty what's full.

— Alice Roosevelt Longworth

Where is your favorite retreat? On a curve of deserted beach, a leafy lakeside hideaway, the summit of a snow-capped peak, a patch of sweeping prairie? We are all stewards of planet earth, with its precious resources entrusted to our care. Whether or not future generations will enjoy these same riches — or whether our own private paradises remain — is up to us, today.

1

Un-Litter the Land

Take a trash bag to a local park, playground, or picnic area and pick up what others have carelessly discarded.

2

Smell the Flowers

If you like to garden, check with local schools, community centers, nursing homes, or hospitals to see if you can plant some perennials to create a bright spot in people's lives.

THOUGHTS THAT COUNT

A firm place to stand is essential, as Archimedes discovered about leverage 2,200 years ago.
With it, we *can* move the world.

— Peter Crosby, president and CEO, SeniorNet

3
Sort It Out

Visit your local recycling center to see what it would take for you to start separating your trash and disposing of it smartly. Start by purchasing a trash container with two or three separate, removable "bins" so that you don't have to sort your recyclables later.

4
Give Yourself a Refill

If you buy bottled drinking water, find out if a local grocery store has a filtered water vending machine where you can refill your empty water bottles for about twenty-five cents per gallon. If your favorite grocer doesn't offer this service, put in a request with the manager.

5

Use It or Refuse It

If you intend to eat your takeout food at home, ask the counter clerk or drive-through provider to hold the napkins, flatware, and condiments you have in your cupboard. If you're calling in your order, make a special request for "no napkins, no flatware, no condiments." Make an effort to patronize establishments that use recycled and recyclable containers for takeout orders.

6

Say It with Pixels

Save a tree by sending electronic greetings for special occasions. You can double your environmental impact with an e-greeting from **care2.com,** where your missive generates support for eco-friendly causes.

7

Shop for Something Green

Whatever you're buying today, it's likely that an environmentally friendly option exists. You can find it online by visiting **greenmatters.com** or **ecomall.com/greenshopping**, or by entering "green shopping" into your favorite Internet search engine.

8

Reuse Your Shoes

Turn your old running shoes into a soccer field, basketball court, or playground. Nike's Reuse-A-Shoe program recycles athletic shoes of any brand — not just Nike shoes — and transforms their materials into athletic surfaces and Nike products. Find a drop-off location at **nikebiz.com** (click on Responsibility, then Environment) or mail shoes to:

NIKE RECYCLING CENTER
c/o Reuse-A-Shoe
26755 SW 95th Avenue
Wilsonville, OR 97070

9
"Green Up" Your Home

Preserve the environment of your own household by buying eco-friendly products for cleaning, pest control, home improvement, lawn care, and more. Find out from the National Institutes of Health's Library of Medicine (**householdproducts.nlm.nih.gov**) what's in your home-care arsenal and whether it's harmful. Environmental Media Services provides suggestions for healthier alternative household cleaners and landscaping practices; visit **ems.org** and click on Library, then topics under Consumer. For more information, contact:

NATIONAL LIBRARY OF MEDICINE
Division of Specialized Information Services
8600 Rockville Pike
Bethesda, MD 20894
E-mail: tehip@teh.nlm.nih.gov

ENVIRONMENTAL MEDIA SERVICES
1320 18th Street NW, 5th Floor
Washington, DC 20036
202-463-6670

10

Put Down Roots

Plant a tree for Arbor Day or to commemorate another event or meaningful occasion. You can start your tree as a tiny seedling in a pot. Ask your local nursery what trees are native to where you live, or take advantage of the resources and fun facts at **arborday.org.**

11

Don't Medicate the Fish

Old or excess medications flushed into sewage systems or discarded where drainage can transport them to waterways can affect aquatic life. Call your pharmacy or local hospital to ask if they collect expired medicines for safe disposal or destruction. If they don't, contact your local hazardous-waste disposal center for instructions.

12

Put Trash on the Wall

Make a poster for your home that lists common materials — aluminum cans, paper, oil-based paints, batteries, motor oil — and how and where you can recycle them. Use the information at **earth911.org,** at your local library, or from your local hazardous-waste disposal center.

13

Order a Refill

Drop off empty printer-ink cartridges at your local office-supply store for recycling.

14

Achieve a Healthy Glow

Use oils and waxes to finish wooden furniture and other items instead of volatile, vaporous polyurethane, lacquer, or varnish.

15

Preserve Public Lands

Annually in September, National Public Lands Day provides a wealth of opportunities around the nation for one-day volunteerism, from cleaning up waterways and restoring habitat to painting park benches and planting sea grass. Find out what you can do by calling 800-865-8337 or visiting **npld.com**.

16

Give Kids Fresh Air

Take a small group of kids on a day hike or other outdoor excursion in your area. Kids from urban locales, in particular, can benefit from connecting with nature.

17

Know Plastic's Number

If you must buy plastic, avoid buying plastics with numbers 3 through 7. (Look for the number inside the embossed triangle on the bottom of most plastic items.) They are difficult to recycle, and their manufacture is very polluting. Be conscious of what types of plastic can be recycled in your area (1 *and* 2?), and buy accordingly.

18

Express Wild Thoughts

Learn about the environmental issues that matter to you, then send an automatic message to your congressional representatives at **saveourenvironment.org.** You can also get tips at the site for writing a letter to your newspaper editor. At **sierraclub.org,** you can send messages to corporations that have environmentally unfriendly practices.

19

Nix Paper and Plastic

Take your own reusable bags to the grocery store; most grocers sell inexpensive, sturdy versions with their name on them. Try to buy products and food with little or no packaging; if you're buying just one produce item, such as a melon, don't bother to bag it in plastic.

20

Surf Active Turf

Introduce a young environmentalist to great Websites with lively games, contests, and activities that teach fun eco-lessons. Enter "kids environment games" into your favorite Web search engine, or try **eddytheeco-dog.com**, **kidsdomain.com/games/earthday.html**, or **missmaggie.org**.

21

Pay Tribute to a Tributary

Find inspiration in the poetry and artwork about watersheds created by young participants in River of Words (**riverofwords.org**). Encourage a young person to enter this annual contest affiliated with the Library of Congress Center for the Book.

22

Choose Friendly Fabric

Look for organic cotton, linen, or industrial hemp instead of rayon. Silk and wool are also good choices. While regular cotton is more forest-friendly than rayon, the pesticides used in growing it cause other environmental problems.

23

Tap Into Good Energy

Find out what products, practices, and energy suppliers in your area will help you save energy and access renewable sources (such as wind, solar, and geothermal energy) at the Energy Guide (**energyguide.com**).

24

Get Reports from the Wilderness

Stay informed with the biweekly Wilderness Support or periodic WildAlerts from the Wilderness Society. Sign up at **wilderness.org** or contact:

THE WILDERNESS SOCIETY
1615 M Street NW
Washington, DC 20036
800-THE-WILD
E-mail: action@tws.org

THOUGHTS THAT COUNT

We all want the same basic things for ourselves and our children — a clean environment, safety, freedom, and equality. But sharing the burden, committing to sustainable living, and considering the multigenerational impact of our actions requires profoundly different thinking from the conventional "wisdom" of today's light-speed world. I, for one, have faith that doing the right thing matters and find the alternative unthinkable, and I think this is how developing better social practices becomes spiritual in nature.

— Seth Heine, founder, CollectiveGood

25
Discover Oceans of Inspiration

Take a trip beneath the ocean to appreciate our undersea treasures. At Oceana (**northamerica.oceana.org**; click on Oceana Interactive), you can look through an ocean-cam, download photos and screensavers of aquatic creatures, get tips on saving beaches, and more. Or find out how many pounds of debris were collected along your state's coastlines during the Ocean Conservancy's annual Coastal Cleanup; see the list at **coastalcleanup.org/results.cfm** or contact:

THE OCEAN CONSERVANCY
1725 DeSales Street NW, Suite 600
Washington, DC 20036
202-429-5609

26

Green-Screen Your Car

Find out how your car ranks in terms of gas mileage (mpg), greenhouse gas emissions, and air pollution ratings at **fueleconomy.gov.** Don't like what you see? Click on Gas Mileage Tips for advice.

27

Give New Life to Old Electronics

CollectiveGood (**collectivegood.com**) recycles your used cell phones and other mobile devices to benefit your choice of more than fifty partner charities. For example, you can drop used cell phones, PDAs (personal digital assistants), and pagers at any Staples store to support the Sierra Club.

CHAPTER TWO

Care about Kids

Do what you can, with what you have,
where you are.

— Theodore Roosevelt

You may have children of your own, you may know some kids on your block, or you may have a child-free life in which "youth" is more a concept than a daily reality. Whatever your circumstances, we all have a stake in how young people grow up, and they rely on us to guide them wisely. By advocating for the health, safety, education, and well-being of children, you pave the way for a productive, promising adulthood — a community that reflects the care given during those early years. Take time to provide attention, engagement, and a listening ear to a young person in need; see what you can do in a day to design a brighter future for a child.

28

Get Parents Talking

Host a group of neighborhood parents to discuss common issues among the kids on the block — even if you don't have kids of your own. A fresh perspective can be invaluable.

29

Share a Story

Read to children at your local library, community center, or child-care center.

30

Open Your Arms to an Infant

Your local hospital needs volunteers to rock babies in its care.

31

Walk Along

Participate in a "walk a child from school" program. Call your local school for information, or organize an informal effort among your neighbors.

THOUGHTS THAT COUNT

When I look into the eyes of the children in Pakistan and Afghanistan, I see my own children. I think that the greatest thing we can do for all of them is to leave them a legacy of peace. This is what motivates me.

— Greg Mortenson, founder and executive director, Central Asia Institute

32
Be a Shelter's Relief

Contact a homeless shelter in your area to ask how you might help with a field trip, picnic, or art workshop for its young residents.

33
Share Your Expertise

Teach what you know — poetry writing, art, crafts, music, theater, nature, computers — at a local youth center or after-school program. Ask the director if you can be part of a special day of "guest instructors."

Form a Friendship

Take an hour or two to value a child in need of extra care. Figure out when you could be available to do any of the following, then contact your neighbor, your church, or your community center and extend your offer to:

- Take a walk together
- Attend a play, movie, sporting event, or school activity
- Work on a creative project together
- Wash the car
- Go grocery shopping, then cook together
- Play catch
- Go to the library
- Go sledding, skating, or snowman-building
- Join a community service project

35
Take Credit for Caring

Apply for the America's Promise credit card. A percentage of your purchases will help fund the work of this national youth-support organization. For more information, visit **americaspromise.org** or contact:

AMERICA'S PROMISE — THE ALLIANCE FOR YOUTH
909 N. Washington Street, Suite 400
Alexandria, VA 22314-1556
703-684-4500

36
Inspire a Shutterbug

Provide a child with a used or new camera and invite him or her to capture life on film. For inspiration, visit the Boys & Girls Clubs of America's ImageMaker's online gallery at **bgca.org** (click on Programs, then The Arts).

37

Provide a Professional Peek

Introduce a secondary school student to a future career via virtual job shadowing. Kids can watch professionals go through a typical day's activities in online videos at **virtualjobshadow.com.** You can also plan for a child to shadow you in person on National Job Shadow Day.

THOUGHTS THAT COUNT

These kids are so smart. Their abilities surpass what I can even imagine. They've grown up with computers. They put an idea on the Internet, and it becomes global. They can really start movements on a grand scale. We're going to see unbelievable things from this generation. We're calling them the Do Something generation.

— Nancy Lublin, founder, Dress for Success, and CEO, Do Something

38
Start with One Thing

Discover 101 *Things You Can Do for Our Children's Future,* a free list available at **connectforkids.org** (click on Volunteer). You can purchase the printed version by calling toll-free: 888-884-1200.

39
Keep Up with Youth

Sign up to receive e-mails about youth issues from the Children's Defense Fund (**childrensdefense.org/getinvolved;** click on Subscribe to an e-mail Listserv under Take Action Online). If you prefer, you can purchase printed materials for a nominal fee at the site's Web Store. For more information:

CHILDREN'S DEFENSE FUND
25 E Street NW
Washington, DC 20001
202-628-8787
E-mail: cdfinfo@childrensdefense.org

40

Develop Character

Tell your school about Operation Respect and its free Don't Laugh at Me programs, which use inspiring music and video recordings along with curriculum guides to teach kids about mutual respect. Programs are tailored to various grade levels, including one for summer camps and after-school programs. Visit **dontlaugh.org** or contact:

OPERATION RESPECT
2 Penn Plaza, 5th Floor
New York, NY 10121
212-904-5243
E-mail: info@operationrespect.org

41

Remember Recess

Find out if KaBOOM has scheduled a playground building or revitalizing project in your area by visiting **kaboom.org.** If not, contact your local youth-support organization, civic leaders, or Home Depot (KaBOOM's official partner) to tell them about the KaBOOM playground building program. When Build Day arrives, pitch in or donate needed tools or materials. For more information:

KABOOM!
2213 M Street NW, Suite 300
Washington, DC 20037
202-659-0215

42

Outfit a Princess

Fairygodmothersinc.com welcomes donations of formal gowns, bridesmaid's dresses, and accessories to outfit underprivileged young women for attending their high school proms. You can mail items to them, or find similar programs in your area by using the site's locator.

FAIRY GODMOTHERS, INC.
c/o Cobra Wire & Cable
2930 Turnpike Drive
Hatboro, PA 19040

43

Mark a Milestone

Depending on the cost, pool resources with a few neighbors and friends to sponsor a high school graduation (cap, gown, portraits) for a child in need.

44
Surprise a Student

Create and send a "care package" to a new college student: brownies or popcorn, a hometown newspaper, photos from home, a movie gift certificate, recorded messages from family and friends.

45
Give Kids Purpose

Involve kids in your community in a project to help other kids. Have them collect gently used children's books from your community and send them to Book-Ends, where they are recycled and placed in schools, shelters, family literacy centers, and youth organizations. Find instructions at **bookends.org** or contact:

BookEnds
6520 Platt Avenue, #331
West Hills, CA 91307
818-716-1198
E-mail: info@bookends.org

Blanket a Baby

If you can knit, crochet, quilt, or complete a fleece or fiber-art baby blanket in a day, you can comfort a vulnerable child. Project Linus provides new, homemade, washable blankets and afghans, created by volunteer blanketeers, to children who are seriously ill, traumatized, or otherwise in need. Find all you need to know at **projectlinus.org** or contact:

PROJECT LINUS
PO Box 5621
Bloomington, IL 61702-5621
309-664-7814
E-mail: information@projectlinus.org

47

Redirect Adrenaline

Ask your local police, fire, and emergency medical teams to host at-risk teens for a day "on the job." Have them emphasize the urgent, action-packed elements of their work so that teens looking for a "rush" can see how those energies can be directed to help others.

48

Provide a Piece of Home

For your next business, community, or social gathering, ask everyone to bring a picture frame. Donate them to a foster-care program and request that each child get one to frame a favorite photo. As children move to new families — some of them repeatedly — they can use this one item to create their own sense of home.

49

Tap Government Sources

Visit **afterschool.gov** for ideas and tips for engaging kids in activities after the school bell rings. At this federally maintained, rich resource, you'll find topics ranging from recreational activities to community service opportunities to advice for adults on starting an after-school program.

THOUGHTS THAT COUNT

Young people make a critical contribution to the social, economic, and democratic development of our society. Now *that* fills me with hope.

— Steven A. Culbertson, president and CEO, Youth Service America

50

Honor a Leader

Nominate a teenager in your community for an award that recognizes his or her accomplishments. Visit your library, consult your schools, or enter "teen achievement awards" into your Web search engine. One example is the American Youth Foundation's "I Dare You" Leadership Award, which honors extraordinary young people for their character and leadership. Recipients receive a $300 scholarship to attend the AYF Leadership Conference in Shelby, Michigan, where they strengthen their leadership skills, develop teamwork, and make lasting friendships. Visit **ayf.com/prog_idy_main.asp** or contact:

AMERICAN YOUTH FOUNDATION
2331 Hampton Avenue
St. Louis, MO 63139
314-646-6000

CHAPTER THREE

Healthy Interest

For in one soul are contained the hopes
and feelings of all Mankind.

— Kahlil Gibran

Some health threats make frequent headlines: AIDS, cancer, heart disease. Others get less press, yet loom much larger when they strike a family member, close friend — or even us. Perhaps you feel moved by a news story about a patient's courageous recovery, or by someone's activism in response to a loved one's lost battle. Whatever the condition, you can help others find hope and healing with these simple acts.

51
Give Blood

To find a blood bank near you, call 800-GIVELIFE or your local hospital, or use the locator on the American Association of Blood Banks' Website (**aabb.org**). You can also schedule an appointment online at **givelife.org**.

52
Get Someone a Free Mammogram

Sponsors and advertisers on **thebreastcancersite.com** provide free mammograms for underprivileged women based on how many people visit the site daily. Surf on over and click on Fund Free Mammograms; it's free, with no obligation to you, and it takes mere seconds. Pass the tip on via your e-mail list to spread the wealth even further.

53
Let Your Mouse Save a Child

Save young lives and help children stay healthy with a click of a button that generates a sponsor's donation. It's completely free to you at **thechildhealthsite.com,** where you'll find daily, monthly, and annual statistics on how many children and which health issues are receiving aid.

54
Affirm Artistic Lives

Browse online galleries featuring the work of various artists who live with AIDS at the Visual AIDS Website (**the body.com/visualaids**).

55
Advocate against AIDS

Join the more than 1,200 volunteer members of Project Inform's Treatment Action Network. TAN members receive e-mail bulletins about hot legislative issues that help them direct letters or phone calls to key policy makers in the fight against AIDS. Sign up at **projectinform.org/org/policy.html** (under Advocacy Resources, click on Treatment Action Network) or contact:

PROJECT INFORM
205 13th Street, #2001
San Francisco, CA 94103
415-558-8669
E-mail: tan@projectinform.org

56
Fund by Phone

Donate your old wireless phone to Sprint Project Connect℠, where a portion of net recycling/reselling proceeds will help raise funds for people with disabilities through Easter Seals and the National Organization on Disability. Drop your phone at a Sprint Store or participating Easter Seals location near you.

57
Arm Yourself with Awareness

Download activity kits with materials for promoting Alcohol Awareness Month, Summer Drinking Awareness, and Holiday Drinking Awareness from the National Council on Alcoholism and Drug Dependence at **ncadd.org/programs/awareness**. Or you can read the organization's fact sheet "Youth, Alcohol and Other Drugs" (**ncadd.org/facts/youthalc.html**) and then order the brochure "What Should I Tell My Child About Drinking?" For more information:

NATIONAL COUNCIL ON ALCOHOLISM
AND DRUG DEPENDENCE
20 Exchange Place, Suite 2902
New York, NY 10005
212-269-7797
E-mail: national@ncadd.org

58

Go to the Dogs

Volunteer for a day at your regional chapter of Canine Companions for Independence (CCI), a nonprofit organization that provides highly trained assistance dogs to people with disabilities. They may need your help in the office, at training graduations, or at other related events. Find a location or subscribe to *The Courier,* CCI's national newsletter, at **caninecompanions.org.**

CANINE COMPANIONS FOR INDEPENDENCE
2965 Dutton Avenue
PO Box 446
Santa Rosa, CA 95402-0446
707-577-1700
E-mail: info@caninecompanions.org

59
Watch Your Wording

Learn to speak with sensitivity about cancer. Gilda's Club (**gildasclub.org**), a support center formed in honor of the late Gilda Radner, advises referring to "people living with cancer," rather than "cancer victims" or "cancer patients." Gilda's Club also recommends encouraging people who live with cancer to express their full range of feelings, rather than insisting on "staying positive."

THOUGHTS THAT COUNT

I believe that one person can change the world, and I see lots of evidence. My cousin, for example, doesn't let his own battle with AIDS keep him from working on behalf of charities and local causes. He is the kind of hero that most of us know. The key to enacting change is inspiring similar action in other people who in turn motivate others to extend the chain.

— Seth Heine, founder, CollectiveGood

60

Move Your Loved Ones

Fight the most widespread health problem in America — obesity — by doing something active with your family today. Take a long walk, bike ride, go hiking. Do jumping jacks until you can't do any more. Set an example for young ones by parking far from the store entrance, taking stairs instead of elevators, walking to destinations within a mile.

61

Be Powerful in Pink

During the month of October, support the fight against breast cancer by wearing a pink ribbon — an act that helps raise awareness and declares your compassion for those living with breast cancer. You'll find instructions for making your own lapel pin (no sewing required) at **cancer.org** (click on Get Involved, then Making Strides Against Breast Cancer, then Make a Pink Ribbon Pin).

62

Affect Health Care Policy

Keep tabs on congressional actions that could affect cancer detection, treatment, and research. Then send an automated message to your representatives. Visit **cancer.org**; click on Get Involved, then Talk to Your Legislators. Or contact:

AMERICAN CANCER SOCIETY
1599 Clifton Road
Atlanta, GA 30329
800-ACS-2345

63

Team Up against Cancer

Tell a basketball coach in your area about the American Cancer Society's Coaches vs. Cancer program, which taps basketball coaches to head up fun, innovative events to raise funds and awareness for the fight against cancer. Visit **cancer.org**; click on Get Involved, then Coaches vs. Cancer.

64

Savor Heart-y Cooking

Ask family and friends to exchange their favorite heart-healthy recipes and compile them into a personal cookbook. Or download some from the recipe-rich resources at the American Heart Association (**americanheart.org**) and share them with family and friends; click on Healthy Lifestyle, then Diet and Nutrition, then Delicious Decisions. For more information:

AMERICAN HEART ASSOCIATION, NATIONAL CENTER
7272 Greenville Avenue
Dallas, TX 75231
800-242-8721

THOUGHTS THAT COUNT

Our nation is changing. The majority is becoming a minority, the elderly population is the fastest growing group, and the gap between rich and poor increases — all this in the most prosperous nation in the world. What can we do? Look for ways to alleviate suffering — and make it a vital part of our everyday lives.

— Patty Johnson, president and CEO,
Rebuilding Together

65

Charge toward a Cure

Register your credit card(s) with the AmeriDollars program to benefit the National Multiple Sclerosis Society or the Skin Cancer Foundation. Every time you shop at a participating merchant, you can choose to have your cash reward rebate donated to the participating charity you designate — at no additional cost to you. Sign up at **ameridollars.com**.

66

Connect Kids with Support

Introduce a child with diabetes or other health challenges to empowering library or online resources. For example, the National Diabetes Association's Youth Zone provides engaging ways to take charge at **diabetes.org/wizdom**. For fun general health activities, try **kidshealth.org** or **kidnetic.com**.

67

Quit with a Kit

Download the "You Can Quit Smoking" kit, a one-stop source to help smokers become tobacco-free, at **ahrq.gov/consumer/tobacco.** You can also order the kit by contacting:

THE U.S. DEPARTMENT OF
HEALTH AND HUMAN SERVICES
200 Independence Avenue SW
Washington, DC 20201
202-619-0257 or 877-696-6775

68

Give Lip Service

Order Sephora's Lip Baume SPF 15 (for men and women) for five dollars at **sephora.com;** enter "lip balm" in the search box. Net proceeds benefit Operation Smile, a not-for-profit medical service organization whose volunteers provide surgery and supplies for repairing burns, tumors, cleft lips and palates, and other birth defects for underprivileged children around the world.

69
Help Someone See

Drop off your old eyeglasses at a LensCrafters in your area; they'll donate them through the Gift of Sight (**givethegiftofsight.org**) program to people in developing countries who need them.

70
Pin Your Hopes on Progress

Call 866-227-7914 for a free "blue star" colon cancer awareness pin. Wearing the pin raises awareness by prompting others to ask what it represents. It also declares your compassion for people living with colon cancer and for finding better treatments or a cure.

CHAPTER FOUR

Sharing Wealth

If you think you are too small to be effective,
you have never been in bed with a mosquito.

— Betty Reese

People who live in poverty struggle against far more than financial lack. Confidence, social participation, and hope for the future can erode as resources dwindle. Everything most of us take for granted, from quality schooling to medical care to appropriate shoes for a job interview, becomes a luxury. Eventually, people without basic means retreat into survival mode as the rest of us go about our comfortable lives. Take a few minutes or an hour to diminish the inequity and revive hope. You can also help people who live in poor conditions by following the suggestions found in chapter 11 (shelter) and chapter 14 (hunger).

71

Put Clothes on Their Backs

Clean out your closet and take all those extra clothes to
the Salvation Army. When winter arrives, gather hats,
mittens, and coats, and drop them off at a local collection
site.

72

Leverage Penny Power

The United Nations' guidelines call for wealthy countries
to contribute 1 percent of their Gross Domestic Product
(GDP) to foreign aid for impoverished countries. Few
nations, including the United States, comply. The Pennies
for Peace campaign urges children to send a letter to Congress supporting a foreign aid budget of 1 percent of GDP.
Attach a penny — 1 percent of a dollar — to point out
that, in Pakistan and Afghanistan, one cent buys a pencil
to help a child learn to read and write. Sample letters are
available at **penniesforpeace.org/sampleletter.html.**

73
Wage War on Inequity

Being informed about minimum wage laws allows us to educate others, become informed voters, and enhance our understanding of related issues. Get "Fast Facts About the Minimum Wage" from the Coalition on Human Needs at **chn.org/issues** (click on Labor and Employment, then Minimum Wage) or write for information:

COALITION ON HUMAN NEEDS
1120 Connecticut Avenue NW, Suite 910
Washington, DC 20036

THOUGHTS THAT COUNT

Generating change for human equality can be a bumpy path. We must take care of ourselves because justice can take time.

— Peter Crosby, president and CEO, SeniorNet

74

Adjust Your Perspective

Read compelling stories written by Peace Corps volunteers about the people and communities they've served; visit **peacecorps.gov/wws/stories** or your local library.

75

Watch Your Words

Be aware of how you speak about the poor in America. Using derogatory terms when talking about low-income families or others who are experiencing poverty dehumanizes people who are struggling with economically difficult situations. If others around you talk insensitively about people in poverty, speak up.

76
Solicit Solutions

Invite a representative from a local antipoverty organization to speak to your PTA, community group, church congregation, or professional association about what's being done to combat poverty in your area. You can search online for "poverty nonprofit organizations" within your city or county or find groups listed under Social Service Organizations in your local Yellow Pages.

77
Argue for Results

Contact your local school and suggest that it host a student debate on living wage laws, affordable housing, gun control, drug control laws, or other issues that affect the lives of people who are living in poor communities. Such a dialogue can generate greater insight into the problems of poverty and reveal potential solutions.

78
Seek Out Scholarship

Help low-income students find college funding sources. Read the newspaper to uncover sources in your own community, and find other opportunities via library research, or on the Internet. One example is the Horatio Alger Association. Visit **horatioalger.com** or contact:

THE HORATIO ALGER ASSOCIATION
99 Canal Center Plaza
Alexandria, VA 22314
703-684-9444

79
Fill a Box

Help send supplies to a family in need by doing your online shopping at The Box Project's "E-store." More than ten million products — apparel, electronics, and more — are available at a 25 percent discount. The Box Project, which provides boxes of food and basic household supplies to struggling families, receives 40 percent of the profits from all products purchased. Visit **boxproject.org**, then shop at **boxproject.theestore.com**.

80

Pass the Test

Take the Catholic Campaign for Human Development's online quiz on poverty in the United States at **usccb.org/cchd/povertyusa/povquiz.htm**. It's easy to do, and the process is enlightening.

THOUGHTS THAT COUNT

In a culture geared toward instant gratification, I see truly making a difference in the world as a realistic, though long-term, proposition. We can't know what the effects of our choices will be generations from now, so our actions require faith. Making a difference also requires discipline. One good deed isn't enough; we need to repeat compassionate acts over time, continuously mindful of others.

— Seth Heine, founder, CollectiveGood

81

Subscribe to Reform

Join the CARE USA Action Network e-mail list. They'll send you information that can help eliminate poverty, as well as tips on urging national leaders to address the crisis of global poverty. Go to **careusa.org** and click on Sign Up Now for the CARE Action Network or write for more information:

CARE USA
151 Ellis Street
Atlanta, GA 30303
800-521-CARE
E-mail: info@care.org

82

Wear Your Heart on Your Wrist

Learn how Doctors Without Borders uses a "Bracelet of Life" to assess the nutritional status of children in impoverished countries. Then visit **doctorswithoutborders.org/ outreach/bol** to download or order your own bracelet and wear it so that you can explain its purpose to everyone who inquires.

83

Bring Scarcity to School

Contact your local school and recommend acquiring the "Access to Essential Medicines" curriculum from Doctors Without Borders, which teaches children about people in developing countries whose lives are devastated by disease and scarce medicines. The free kit includes six suggested lesson plans, a short documentary film, copies of *It's a Different World Without Medicines* magazine, roleplaying cards, and more. The kit can be downloaded (without the film) or ordered online at **doctorswithout borders.org/education/science_life/teachers.** Or you may contact:

DOCTORS WITHOUT BORDERS
333 7th Avenue, 2nd Floor
New York, NY 10001-5004
212-679-6800

84

Outfit a New Employee

Donate gently used professional work clothing and accessories to organizations that help low-income men and women get and keep jobs. Look for a collection site under Social Service Organizations in your local Yellow Pages, or visit **careergear.org** (for men) and **dressforsuccess.org** (for women) for drop-off and mailing instructions.

85

Give Old PCs New Purpose

When you upgrade, donate your used computer and equipment to the National Cristina Foundation, which gives computers to public service organizations that provide education and training to people who are economically disadvantaged. Visit **cristina.org** or call 203-863-9100.

86

Motivate with Merchandise

Drop your gently used clothing and household goods at your local Goodwill Industries location, where their sale will fund job training, employment services, and post-employment support for people striving for economic independence. Visit **goodwill.org** for more information, including the nearest location, or contact:

GOODWILL INDUSTRIES INTERNATIONAL, INC.
15810 Indianola Drive
Rockville, MD 20855
301-530-6500

87

Trade Ink for Aid

Donate your used printer cartridges to Recycling for the Poor, who will deliver them to a paying recycler. Proceeds are used to obtain food, housing, medical aid, and other services. Refillable cartridges are worth two to four dollars each, and organization leaders say that two dollars buys twenty pounds of rice and beans, which can feed eighty children. For maximum impact, get your workplace in on the effort. To receive a free, postage-paid shipping container from Recycling for the Poor, visit **foodforthepoor.org/recycle** or contact:

FOOD FOR THE POOR, INC.
550 SW 12th Avenue, Department 9662
Deerfield Beach, FL 33442
954-427-2222 or 800-427-9104

CHAPTER FIVE

Keeping Peace

We don't know who we are until
we see what we can do.

— Martha Grimes

Violence takes many forms, from gang wars and street riots to child abuse and common road rage. Even the bully on the playground inflicts a unique brand of assault. Few condone violence, but many who participate give it other names: justice, payback, discipline, control, stress, bullying. No matter the term, we are all vulnerable — and accountable. Take a moment today to unearth alternatives to violence and clear a path to peace.

88

Keep an Eye Out

Participate in a neighborhood watch program or a security walk (or drive) for an evening. Contact your local police department for information.

89

Comfort Sheltered Families

Put together care boxes for women and children staying in domestic violence centers. (Find the centers listed under Social Service Organizations in your Yellow Pages.) Include gently used toys for the children. Deliver to your area shelter, or mail them if your town doesn't have one.

If we take one step at a time, whether to reduce gun violence or advocate for the disabled, we can make our world a better place.

— Sarah Brady, chair,
The Brady Campaign to End Gun Violence

90

Recognize Peacekeepers

Suggest to the leaders of your community center or place of worship that they nominate and then honor a local citizen each year for his or her antiviolence efforts in your community.

91

Provide a Lifeline

Donate an old cell phone — even a broken one — to help victims of domestic violence make critical calls. The Wireless Foundation works with Motorola and the National Coalition Against Domestic Violence to recondition some phones and reprogram them to dial emergency numbers. The phones and free airtime are then given to women in jeopardy. Other phones are recycled and resold to help fund agencies that work to end domestic violence. Visit **donateaphone.com** for collection points in your area or mail your phone (and the charger and battery if you have them) to:

CALL TO PROTECT
2555 Bishop Circle West
Dexter, MI 48130-1563

92
Fight Fair

Do arguments with your spouse or partner escalate into yelling, obscenities, slamming doors, or even throwing things? Are your children witnesses? Learn to disagree more calmly and rationally. For tips on how to do this, visit **conflict911.com/resources/Fighting_Fair.**

93
Start a Parenting Revolution

Ask a parenting group or other community group to devote a daylong meeting to the topic of raising compassionate sons. Invite speakers to discuss not just domestic violence, sexual assault, and date rape, but also more subtle forms of disrespect and devaluation.

94
Get It on Film

Donate a video or photo camera to an organization that documents violence around the world. Enter "donate camcorder activists" into your favorite Web search engine or try RAWA (Revolutionary Association of Women in Afghanistan) at **rawa.org.**

95
Shift Power

Learn about the vital role men can play in preventing rape and other violence against women. Enter "men against rape" into your favorite Web search engine or go to **mencanstoprape.org.** Reprint the information in your organization's or faith community's newsletter, or download fact sheets and distribute them in your community. For more information, contact:

MEN CAN STOP RAPE
PO Box 57144
Washington, DC 20037
202-265-6530
E-mail: info@mencanstoprape.org

96
Break the Cycle

Tell your middle and high schools, community youth groups, and juvenile detention centers about Break the Cycle's innovative curriculum, "Ending Violence: A Curriculum for Educating Teens on Domestic Violence and the Law." "Ending Violence" is an interactive program that uses visual aids, games, and role-playing to engage and educate students. To find out more, visit **break-the-cycle.org** (click on Our Programs) or contact:

BREAK THE CYCLE
PO Box 64996
Los Angeles, CA 90064
310-286-3366 or 888-988-TEEN
E-mail: info@break-the-cycle.org

97

Arm Yourself with Knowledge

Become informed about the gun laws are in your state. Visit **atf.treas.gov/firearms/statelaws** or write to your state legislators. Then order a free "Stop 2" kit from The Brady Center to Prevent Gun Violence and share it with your area schools, faith community, civic organization, or community center. Visit **bradycenter.org/stop2** or contact:

THE BRADY CENTER TO PREVENT GUN VIOLENCE
1225 Eye Street NW, Suite 1100
Washington, DC 20005
202-289-7319

THOUGHTS THAT COUNT

Activism is an opportunity to make connections with people we never would meet otherwise. It's a wonderful way to celebrate life.

— Sarah Brady, chair,
The Brady Campaign to End Gun Violence

98
Help Stylists Spot Trouble

Help domestic violence victims by telling your hair stylist about Cut It Out, a national program that builds awareness of domestic abuse and trains salon professionals to recognize warning signs and safely refer clients to local resources. Salons can order posters and safety card kits and inquire about training sessions by visiting **cutitout.org.**

99
Show Solidarity

Whenever you learn that someone in your community has been a victim of a hate crime, write a letter or place a phone call in support of that person — if not directly to the victim, then to the local newspaper.

100

Let Kids Picture Peace

Ask schools, civic leaders, church groups, or businesses to sponsor an antiviolence poster or essay contest in your community — or you can hold one among your neighborhood kids.

101

Make Practical Choices

Understand the ways in which gun ownership can put you and your family at risk. For instance, many states hold parents liable for their children's actions, including inappropriate use of firearms — not to mention actions that people who are injured may take against you.

102

Break Up Bad Dates

Help prevent teen dating violence by learning to recognize the signs. According to the National Crime Prevention Council, these include:

- Acting jealous and possessive
- Trying to control by being bossy, giving orders, and making all the decisions
- Having a history of fighting or mistreating others
- Abusing alcohol or other drugs
- Pressuring a partner for sex or acting forceful about sex
- Selecting a partner's friends
- Deciding what a partner wears

Find more information at **ncpc.org** (enter "teen dating" into the Search Our Site box) or contact:

NATIONAL CRIME PREVENTION COUNCIL
1000 Connecticut Avenue NW, 13th Floor
Washington, DC 20036
202-466-6272

103

Round Up Local Resources

Create and distribute to your entire neighborhood a resource list for family support to ward off problems before they escalate. Include:

- Parent-education programs that teach child development and parenting skills
- Home-visiting programs that provide social support, education, and crisis intervention
- Substance-abuse treatment programs
- Well-baby and child-care programs
- Respite care for families with a child or other family member who is ill or who has a disability
- Conflict and anger management courses or counseling
- Homes with parental supervision where kids are welcome to gather after school

104

Print Out Some Prevention

Download, copy, and distribute free brochures from the National Crime Prevention Council on topics such as Community Crime Prevention, Conflict Resolution/Anger Management, Sexual Assault, and Child Safety, among others. Find them at **ncpc.org** or contact:

NATIONAL CRIME PREVENTION COUNCIL
1000 Connecticut Avenue NW, 13th Floor
Washington, DC 20036
202-466-6272

105

Don't Be a Bystander

Take what you hear seriously. If you hear or know of someone planning to harm neighbors or the community in any way, report it to law enforcement immediately.

106

Encourage Young Crime-Fighters

Introduce a child to **McGruff.org,** where games and other online interactive resources entertain while educating them about safety, conflict resolution, crime solving, and more.

107

Curb Road Rage

Drive with patience and tolerance. Keep the peace on our streets and highways, and set a good example for your passengers.

108

Rescue a Child

Recognize the warning signs of possible child abuse or neglect:

- Nervousness around adults
- Aggression toward adults or other children
- Inability to stay awake or to concentrate for extended periods
- Sudden dramatic changes in personality or activities
- Acting out sexually or showing interest in sex that is not age-appropriate
- Frequent or unexplained bruises or injuries
- Low self-esteem
- Poor hygiene

If you are concerned that a child is being harmed, call child protective services (listed in your local phone book), your local police department, or Childhelp USA® at 800-4-A-CHILD.

109

Stand against Stalkers

Know what to do if you or someone you know becomes the focus of a stalker. Ask a representative from your local police department to speak to the issue at your community or educational group's next meeting. Access the resources of the National Center for Victims of Crime at **ncvc.org/src** or contact:

NATIONAL CENTER FOR VICTIMS OF CRIME
Stalking Resource Center
2000 M Street NW, Suite 480
Washington, DC 20036
202-467-8700
E-mail: src@ncvc.org

110

Keep the Toy Chest Weapon-Free

Look for alternatives to toys that promote or glorify shooting and other violence. Rather than endorse action figures that rely on weaponry and brute strength, introduce your child to mystery-solving games, medical and lifesaving accessories, nature kits, and simple cameras or camcorders — and the related heroism of police detectives, emergency medical teams, global preservationists, photojournalists, and documentary filmmakers.

111

Ban Bullying

In the adult world, physical bullying is called assault and it's against the law. Treat attacks among youths with the same seriousness. Ask administrators whether your school provides confidential means for students to report harassment or bullying. Encourage school administrators to adopt Internet-use policies that address online hate and harassment. Explain to kids that name-calling and teasing are not acceptable behaviors, and that they can easily escalate into fistfights — or worse. Point out that even when the teaser has no violent intentions, the victim may react with force.

112

Spare the Rod

If you aren't yet convinced that spanking isn't the best way to discipline a child, consider the contradictory message that pro-spanking parents send if they also teach children that hitting is wrong and hurtful. At the very least, arm yourself with alternatives; the Center for Effective Discipline lists some at **stophitting.com/spankOut/ effectiveDisciplineTips.php.** If you're already an advocate of alternatives, you can help spread the message by getting the list published in your church bulletin or the newsletter of your community group or member organization. For more information:

CENTER FOR EFFECTIVE DISCIPLINE
155 West Main Street, Suite 1603
Columbus, OH 43215
614-221-8829

113

Be a Good Sport

If your child competes in sports, remind yourself and your child that the goal is personal growth, pride, and teamwork — not winning at all costs or yielding to anger. Speak up if the coach uses angry yelling, confrontation, or physical force to "motivate" players. If parents or other spectators react with aggression or obscenities, ask the sponsoring entity to distribute and enforce a written policy that such behavior won't be tolerated at their venue.

CHAPTER SIX

Conscious Consumerism

When you make a world tolerable for yourself,
you make a world tolerable for others.

— Anaïs Nin

In our commercial culture, our attention is continually diverted toward material acquisition, and our purchasing decisions endorse or decry how companies conduct their business. Choosing where you spend your dollars — or whether to spend them at all — can reflect your values about child and slave labor, corporate integrity, environmental protection, animal welfare, global market inequities, and more. Here are some simple ways to invest your dollars with greater positive influence.

114
Brew a Better World

Learn about fair-trade coffee and how your purchase helps fight poverty and environmental degradation; find information at **globalexchange.org**. Ask your favorite coffee supplier if they offer fair-trade coffee or look for "fair trade" labeling on packages.

115
Dress for Workers' Success

Buy sweatshop-free and union-made clothing to support companies that maintain fair labor standards for workers around the globe. For resources, visit **newdream.org/consumer/clothing.html** or contact:

CENTER FOR A NEW AMERICAN DREAM
6930 Carroll Avenue, #900
Takoma Park, MD 20912
301-891-3683 or 877-68-DREAM
E-mail: newdream@newdream.org

116

Feed Local Farming

Support local farms — and small farmers who are struggling against agribusiness giants — by buying local food at farmers' markets, produce stands, and your local supermarket. If you don't see signs or labels at your grocery store, ask the manager if they carry local produce; if not, explain why you would prefer to buy locally grown food. Spread the word when you find a store that sells locally produced goods. For more information about buying locally grown food, ask your local librarian to suggest some resources, enter "buying local" into your favorite Web search engine, download the Food and Farm Toolkit from **oxfamamerica.org** (click on Publications, then Organizing/Advocacy Tools), or contact:

OXFAM AMERICA
26 West Street
Boston, MA 02111
800-77-OXFAM or 617-482-1211
E-mail: info@oxfamamerica.org

117

Check Your Charity

Research charities before giving them your money or your support. Check with your local librarian or visit Guidestar (**guidestar.org**), the Internet Nonprofit Center (**nonprofits.org/lib**), the Wise Giving Alliance (**give.org**), or Charity Navigator (**charitynavigator.org**).

118

Support Social Consciousness

Make purchases from socially conscious businesses, such as Working Assets, Greystone Bakery, and Newman's Own, which give a portion of their earnings to communities and good causes. Identify other such businesses by entering "socially conscious business" into your favorite Web search engine.

119

Practice Commercial-Free Citizenship

Resist arguments that link your patriotism to shopping. Show your gratitude for your freedom in other ways.

120

Give Greater Gifts

Be a conscious gift-giver and receiver. Shop online at charity malls, where a percentage of your purchases is donated to the charity you choose. Or direct those who'll be giving *you* gifts for a special occasion to a charitable Website that arranges donations. Enter "charity mall" into your favorite Web search engine or try **iGive.com, altgifts.org,** or **charitygift.com.**

121

Revise Your Media Menu

Just as you might assess your eating habits, consider adjusting your (and your family's) media habits as well. The George Lucas Educational Foundation (**glef.org**) suggests devising a "media diet" that balances how much and what kind of media you're exposed to daily, paired with analysis and discussion. For more information:

GEORGE LUCAS EDUCATIONAL FOUNDATION
PO Box 3494
San Rafael, CA 94912
415-507-0399
E-mail: edutopia@glef.org

122

Keep Chocolate Sweet

Buy fair-trade chocolate so that African cocoa farmers are paid equitably, eliminating the use of child and slave labor from poor countries. Look for "Fair Trade Certified" labels, which guarantee a minimum price to growers and ensure that no child or forced labor is used.

123

Demand Better Terms

Consider language. Think about how often you are referred to as a "consumer" and what that means, literally.

THOUGHTS THAT COUNT

Can one person really make a difference in the world? The classic answer, from Margaret Mead, is, "It's the only thing that ever has."

— Nancy Lublin, founder, Dress for Success, and CEO, Do Something

---

124

Unfill a Landfill

Learn to fix and refurbish things instead of automatically replacing them. If you don't have time to do the work yourself, take repairable goods to a professional who can do the job for you.

125

Know Your Labels

For eco-friendly products, look for the Green Seal or Scientific Certification Systems labels, or other labels offered by respected environmental organizations. For wood products, check for certification by the Forest Stewardship Council (FSC). For seafood, look for Marine Stewardship Council (MSC) certification. For coffee, environmental responsibility is reflected in "organic" and "shade grown" labeling.

126

Get the Picture

Watch online video clips at **newdream.org/consumer/video.html** that show how current global economic practices increase the gap between the wealthy and the impoverished. Or visit your local video store to rent the documentary DVD "Life & Debt" for a look at Jamaica's experience with free trade.

127

Aim Marketing at Mature Audiences

Write to your congressperson to oppose aggressive marketing to children, who are too young to make informed buying decisions. To learn more, visit **commercialalert.org;** click on Government, then Federal Trade Commission. Or contact:

COMMERCIAL ALERT
4110 S.E. Hawthorne Boulevard, #123
Portland, OR 97214-5426
503-235-8012

128

Protest Pint-Sized Sales

Suggest noncommercial fund-raisers for your local schools so that kids don't end up selling things that people don't want or need. Suggest a school fair, film night, arts festival, or silent auction instead.

129

Raise Conscious Kids

Order or download the thirty-two-page booklet "Tips for Parenting in a Commercial Culture" at **newdream.org** or contact:

CENTER FOR A NEW AMERICAN DREAM
6930 Carroll Avenue, #900
Takoma Park, MD 20912
301-891-3683 or 877-68-DREAM
E-mail: newdream@newdream.org

130

Grow a Wise Buyer

Teach your child how to make smart buying decisions when you're shopping for birthday presents for other kids. Ask your child to consider whether a potential gift will have more than one purpose, if it will still be "fun" months later, if it requires additional purchases (batteries, software), and whether it might break easily.

131

Declare a Day Off

Participate in Buy Nothing Day each year in November — or on the day of your choice. Traditionally observed on Black Friday — the day after American Thanksgiving and the busiest shopping day of the year — Buy Nothing Day advocates retreating for twenty-four hours from our frenzied commercial culture. Recognize that keeping your wallet closed can be more about gain than loss.

132

Trade Cash for a Good Conscience

Affirm your values with your dollars. For the products you buy routinely, find out which manufacturers have the most reputable business practices at **responsibleshopper.org.** Or contact:

CO-OP AMERICA
1612 K Street NW, Suite 600
Washington, DC 20006
800-584-7336

133

Invest in Your Beliefs

Learn about socially responsible investing before you pick a retirement fund or other investment opportunity. Ask your financial institution or adviser, enter "social investing" into your favorite Web search engine, or visit the Social Investment Forum at **socialinvest.org.**

134

Add Value Online

Care2's "Green Thumbs-Up" is a small, free software program that automatically generates donations as you surf or shop with Care2's business affiliates. Care2 receives a commission from the sale — from 1 percent to 12.5 percent — and donates the entire amount to environmental organizations. The program also identifies companies that use labor- and environment-unfriendly practices — and those that earn high marks for social consciousness — according to **responsibleshopper.org** and the Green Pages Online (**greenpages.org**). Sign up at **care2.com/greenthumb**.

THOUGHTS THAT COUNT

One of the greatest rewards of my job is the chance to meet people of conscience who have taken some of these steps. I meet them every day, and that gives me hope that broad social change is within our reach if each one of us takes action.

— Wayne Pacelle, president and CEO,
The Humane Society of the United States

135
Reward Originality

Shop at a local, independently owned store or dine at a locally owned restaurant instead of a chain at least once a week. Buying from local merchants does more than simply support small, independent businesses. Shopping locally strengthens the local economy by keeping dollars circulating within the community, and it lends greater variety and more character to shopping districts. Local business can also be easier on the environment if it is less reliant on long-distance truck delivery.

CHAPTER SEVEN

Common Humanity

Be a beacon. Beacons of light are calm,
steady, and consistent.

— Joan R. Tarpley

"Tolerance" is the term commonly used to describe the harmony of people of all races, genders, faiths, cultures, and sexual orientations. But simply tolerating someone falls far short of valuing that person's singular character and embracing all you have in common. The world is home to 6.4 billion people; we can never know them all, but surely we are enriched by keeping our hearts and minds open to every person whose path intersects with our own. We have much to learn from each other, and much to gain.

136
Worship with the World

Share spiritual community and broaden your world by attending services at a church, synagogue, or temple of a faith other than your own.

137
Open Eyes with Arts

Attend a play, listen to music, or go to a dance performance by artists whose race or ethnicity is different from your own.

138

Collect Tolerance Tips

Visit **tolerance.org** and order or download the site's free information sources: "101 Tools for Tolerance," "10 Ways to Fight Hate," "10 Ways to Fight Hate on Campus," and "Responding to Hate at School."

139

Tap Youthful Wisdom

Invite young children to paint pictures of their faces, using whatever blend of colors they think represents their skin tone. Ask them to name the color they made their face. (Notice that they aren't likely to say "black" or "white.")

140

Engage in International Commerce

Shop at ethnic grocery stores, specialty markets, and other minority-owned businesses. Get to know the owners. Ask about their family histories.

141

Expand Your Vocabulary

Learn how to say "Hello," "How are you," and other common friendly phrases in another language that is spoken in your community. Take every opportunity to communicate with non-English-speaking neighbors.

142

Give Words Weight

Speak up when you hear slurs. When someone asks if you're offended by racial or ethnic jokes, say "yes." If someone tells such a joke or makes similar comments at a social gathering, explain that you prefer not to hear those types of remarks. Deliver your response with a light touch so that the speaker can recover with dignity intact. If he or she persists, consider leaving the room.

143

Diversify

Make a list of your friends, coworkers, and acquaintances and their respective races, religions, and ethnicities. If your list looks a little homogeneous, invite someone of a different background to a party or a meal.

144

Expand Entertainment Horizons

Read a book or watch a movie about another culture.

145

Know What Kids Watch

View movies, TV shows, computer games, and other media with your children; point out stereotypes and cultural misinformation that you see.

THOUGHTS THAT COUNT

Although Women Transcending Boundaries came together initially to support the Muslim women in our community, we wanted to know more about all faiths; all of us learned we have more in common than we imagined.

— Betsy Wiggins, cofounder,
Women Transcending Boundaries

Cultivate a World View

Choose schools, day-care centers, after-school programs, and camps that provide opportunities for kids to meet others from different backgrounds. If your neighborhood is culturally and economically homogeneous, find other ways, such as cultural festivals or weekend road trips, to expose your family to different ways of living.

147

Confirm Safety Nets

Ask your area schools what type of support they offer to gay and lesbian youth. If you aren't satisfied with the answer, supply informational materials, such as those provided by the Gay, Lesbian, and Straight Education Network (**glsen.org**).

148

Rally Around Common Causes

Identify a concern in your community that is shared among *all* citizens. Ask civic or faith communities to organize a daylong volunteer event to resolve it, with representation from many groups. Clean up a park or waterway, paint a school or community center, build a public playground, or plant a peace garden.

149

Set a Special Table

Host a potluck dinner featuring authentic recipes from another culture. If you can, include authentic table settings and serving traditions.

150

Invite Nonlocal Color

Ask local museums and galleries to host exhibits and events that reflect cultures beyond your community.

151

Adopt a Global Perspective

Watch or listen to the BBC or other international broadcasters' news for a less U.S.-centered perspective of world events. (Check your TV and radio listings for stations and times.)

152

Click into Inclusiveness

Introduce a child to a Website where games and stories teach kids to embrace inclusion. Enter "kids peace advocates" into your favorite Web search engine or try **celebratingpeace.com.**

153

Fly a Colorful Kite

With kids, read *The Kite Story,* then build a Peace Kite. Visit **unesco.org/education;** click on Non-Violence Education, then The Kite Story.

154
Read around the World

Read books with multicultural and inclusive themes to your children. Consult the National Education Association's Website for recommended books with Asian-American, Native American, African-American, and Spanish/ English/Bilingual themes. Also of interest is the NEA's "50 Multicultural Books Every Child Should Know." Visit **nea.org** and click on NEA's Read Across America.

155
Share the Dream

Read about Dr. Martin Luther King's "Beloved Community" and his vision for a just and peaceful world at **thekingcenter.com** or your local library.

156

Expand Your Religious Experience

Can you name the five major religions of the world? Learn more about world religions — particularly what they have in common — either online or at your local library.

157

Explore Living History

One of the most powerful ways to learn history is to talk with someone who has lived it. Ask a friend over the age of sixty who is of another race or religion — or a family member from another nation or culture — to describe his or her experiences growing up.

158

Watch Over Human Rights

Choose a campaign that opposes racial violence from the list at Human Rights Watch (**hrw.org**) and take one of the recommended actions, from writing a letter to officials, to reading more about the topic, to volunteering professional services. Past campaigns have addressed violence against gay students and military attacks against minority populations around the world.

THOUGHTS THAT COUNT

It started with *just one person* making a phone call, asking how to help. Now Women Transcending Boundaries is a unique, dynamic group of women dedicated to educating ourselves and our community about our diverse religious and spiritual traditions. We are personally enriched by hearing one another's stories, learning about each other's faith and culture, and sharing our common concerns. Our dialogue is helping to break the cycle of ignorance and suffering and move beyond boundaries toward hope.

— Betsy Wiggins, cofounder,
Women Transcending Boundaries

CHAPTER EIGHT

Arts Afire

You don't have to sit on top of a mountain
to discover what's right for you. You always
know in your heart what you need to do.

— Liz Dolan

Whether through writing, painting, dance, music, theater, or other media, the arts enrich our lives in countless ways and provide the stage for creative talent to flourish. Young people in particular benefit from discovering avenues of expression that engage their imaginations and individual energies. Yet arts education is increasingly vulnerable — and sometimes nonexistent — as school budgets are stretched thin. Take a stand to preserve the inspirational power and potential of the arts.

159
Color a Child's Walls

Revel in your own riches and cheer a struggling child by enrolling in "Accounting Your Blessings," an e-mail-based exercise in gratitude offered by Artella, an online support community for artists, writers, and other creative spirits. Artella donates one dollar of every five dollar enrollment fee to Artists Helping Children, a nonprofit group that comforts children in hospitals, clinics, and shelters by brightening their environment with murals and other art. Visit **artellawordsandart.com/difference.html** and sign up for "Accounting Your Blessings"

THOUGHTS THAT COUNT

Everybody has a strength to share. Everybody's been given a gift of some type, and if we can tap into that, if we can create vehicles in which people can contribute whatever their particular unique talent or gift is, then that can really change the world.

— Bill Shore, founder and executive director, Share Our Strength

160

Show Up for Free

Attend arts and cultural events in your locale whenever you can; it's enriching for you, and beneficial to the artists and the event sponsors. Art openings, craft shows, concerts, poetry readings, and performances are often free for the enjoying. Check your local newspaper for events or visit venues or their Websites and sign up for their mailing lists.

161

Take Art to School

Find out what type of arts education is available in your local schools. Write letters to your newspapers and your congressional representatives explaining why arts education is vital to young minds. Back up your position with information from The Arts Education Partnership (**aep-arts.org**).

162

Publicize Artistry

Help spread the word about community arts events by posting notices on public bulletin boards, in e-mails to friends, and in group newsletters.

163

Create Artful Government

Learn about arts-related legislation and what you can do in response at **artsusa.org/issues/advocacy** or contact:

AMERICANS FOR THE ARTS
1000 Vermont Avenue NW, 6th Floor
Washington, DC 20005
202-371-2830

164

Make Art Newsworthy

Create a contact list of local and regional arts resources. Include support organizations, arts venues, theater and dance companies, art galleries, publications, educational programs, teachers, and more. Ask your local newspaper to print the list.

165

Mix Your Media

Spend some time watching and listening to arts-related media. Your PBS (Public Broadcasting System) station features programming in every area of the arts; the cable TV station C-SPAN carries presentations by and interviews with authors; NPR (National Public Radio) broadcasts several programs with arts news and commentary. If you already tune in, expand your horizons; try a program about a topic that's unfamiliar to you.

166

Welcome Artistic E-mail

Sign up for the free e-newsletter of Americans for the Arts at **americansforthearts.org**.

THOUGHTS THAT COUNT

One person *can* make a difference in the world. As we have become technologically advanced, our fast-paced society has lost touch with the concept of listening to our hearts. We make decisions based on logic, not intuition. Often, when I ask people in Afghanistan why they are doing something, they answer, "because my heart told me to." We would do well to subscribe to the old saying, "When your heart speaks, take good notes."

— Greg Mortenson, founder and executive director, Central Asia Institute

167

Exhibit Your Town

Provide an art show for your community by appealing to civic leaders' own artistic talents. Ask them to consider hosting a National Arts Program exhibit. These free exhibits, held annually around the nation, invite municipal employees and their families (with others included at their discretion) to contribute their artwork for public display, welcoming all ages, backgrounds, and levels of talent. In addition to the artwork, host communities provide a program coordinator, exhibit site(s), and judges. The National Arts Program Foundation provides an organizing handbook and rules, registration and promotional materials, cash awards, and other support. For more information, contact:

THE NATIONAL ARTS PROGRAM FOUNDATION
699 Sugartown Road
Malvern, PA 19355
610-408-9600
ntlartsprog.org

168

Serve an Art-Minded Audience

Volunteer to take tickets, serve as an usher, or sell merchandise at a theatrical or musical performance in your community.

169

Read to Feed an Artist

Are you shopping for an art-related or soul-inspiring book? Check out the recommendations on the National Association of Independent Artists' Website (**naia-artists.org/resources/amazon.htm**). If you click on the link that takes you to **amazon.com** to buy a book, a percentage of the sale goes to support the NAIA.

170
Put Art on the Menu

Suggest that your workplace display the work of a local artists' group on its walls or in a designated break area. Ask restaurants in your community to exhibit the work of local artists on their walls on a rotating basis.

171
Share National Resources

Encourage teachers in your local schools and other educators you may know to download a free Educator Resource Pack from the Corcoran Gallery of Art, entitled "In Response to Place: Photographs from the Nature Conservancy's Last Great Places." You'll find it at **corcoran.org/education/class_material.htm.** (Other Resource Pack topics are available for DC-area teachers to borrow.) You may also contact:

THE CORCORAN GALLERY OF ART
500 17th Street NW
Washington, DC 20006
202-639-1700

172

Buy Some Influence

Do your online shopping at **Buyforcharity.com,** where up to 35 percent of your purchase amount will support the arts organizations you designate from the site's list of over 120 recipients.

173

Put Yourself to Artful Work

Call an arts group in your community and ask what you can help them with in a day. You might end up stuffing envelopes for film society members, distributing posters for the community theater's performance, calling potential donors for the art league, or compiling reviews of the choral group's last performance.

174
Nurture a Virtual Artist

Introduce a child to a Website that fires his or her artistic imagination with projects, games, and education. Go to Art Kids Rule (**artkidsrule.com**), The Art Room (**arts.ufl.edu/art/rt_room**), or Scribbles Kids Art Site (**scribbleskidsart.com**) — or enter "kids art fun online" in your favorite Web search engine. You can also find great resources at your local library.

175
Hire an Aspiring Artist

Write a letter to arts-oriented businesses in your community encouraging them to hire youth interns from your local high school or community center — or help a teenager write a letter requesting such an internship. Working for a photo studio, graphic design agency, or literary magazine can be a great way for young people from all backgrounds to find not only creative expression, but also an eventual source of income.

176

Invite Student Submissions

Ask your local PTA to sponsor the annual arts Reflections Program, which encourages students to create works of art for fun and recognition. Students (preschool through grade twelve) can submit entries in four areas: literature, musical composition, photography, and the visual arts (including drawing, painting, printmaking, and collage). For more information, call your local PTA or visit **pta.org/parentinvolvement/familyfun/aboutreflect.asp.**

177

Pass on the Present

Are you celebrating a birthday, anniversary, or other gift-getting occasion? Pick an arts-related organization you admire and ask gift-givers to make donations to that organization instead of giving you stuff.

Jazz Up Your Inner Altruist

Read about the inspiring work of the Jazz Foundation of America (**jazzfoundation.org**), an organization that helps aging musicians — whose careers leave them without retirement benefits, health insurance, or other means of support — pay their living expenses. For fun, play your own tune on the cyber keyboard at the foundation's Website for a reminder of what these talented artists contribute to our culture. For more information, contact:

JAZZ FOUNDATION OF AMERICA
322 West 48th Street, 3rd Floor
New York, NY 10036
212-245-3999
E-mail: jazzfoundation@rcn.com

CHAPTER NINE

Honoring Elders

We can do no great things —
only small things with great love.

— Mother Teresa

Despite their long, productive lives, unique perspectives, and rich experiences, older Americans often become virtually invisible to the rest of society. Other cultures treat their elder citizens with much greater respect and dignity, treasuring the accumulated wisdom and achievement that the years bestow. You can move our culture in a healthier direction by taking a few moments to reach out and form an intergenerational bond. Here are some simple actions you can take to enrich the life of an elder citizen — and, in the process, enrich your own.

179
Record a Riveting Tale

Tape-record yourself reading a story for someone who can no longer see the fine print.

180
Preserve Personal History

Visit a nursing home and tape-record a resident's tale of a life well lived. Transcribe it and send copies to the nursing home and, if you can find out their addresses, to family members. You might also make a collage or shadow box that represents the person's memories and present it to him or her.

181

Help Tell a Story

Donate large-print reading materials and books on tape to hospitals, senior centers, nursing homes, and retirement homes.

182

Drive It Home

Contact your area's Meals on Wheels program to see if they need delivery help.

THOUGHTS THAT COUNT

We need to cooperate on a more fundamental level, to make sacrifices for people we don't even know, expecting that they will reciprocate. Perhaps they won't, but the effects of the practice itself, like the ripples in a pond, radiate outward.

— Seth Heine, founder, CollectiveGood

183

Help a Grandparent Parent

Tell a grandparent about *Parenting Grandchildren: A Voice for Grandparents,* a free newsletter from the American Association of Retired Persons (AARP) Grandparent Information Center. Mailed through the U.S. Postal Service, the newsletter provides help to grandparents who are raising their grandchildren. Sign up at **aarp.org/life/grandparents** (click on Grandparent Information Center, then look for the newsletter box with link) or contact:

AARP GRANDPARENT INFORMATION CENTER
601 E Street NW
Washington, DC 20049
888-OUR-AARP
E-mail: gic@aarp.org

184

Feed a Friend

Many low-income seniors go hungry. Ask your local newspaper, church bulletins, and senior center newsletters to feature a story about community resources available for seniors, such as food pantries and meal sites.

185

Pitch In Personally

Volunteer for a day at your local senior center. They might need you to type, stuff envelopes, or conduct online research. You can also share what you know, whether your field is health care, nutrition, consumer protection, or finances.

186

Weave a Supportive Web

Introduce a senior to the Internet, where a wealth of resources is available, including message boards and chat rooms where they can find common ground. Start with **seniornet.org** and follow its links for more resources. Bookmark their favorite pages for them.

187

Harness the Law Online

Learn about legal issues affecting seniors at the National Senior Citizens Law Center, including health care, assisted living, and retirement income. Visit **nsclc.org** or contact:

NATIONAL SENIOR CITIZENS LAW CENTER
1101 14th Street NW, Suite 400
Washington, DC 20005
202-289-6976

188

Capture a Theme

A life-affirming photo is a powerful way to honor a person. Take a thoughtfully composed photograph of an older person that reflects the designated annual theme of Older Americans Month. (Visit the Administration on Aging at **aoa.gov/press/oam/oam.asp** to find out this year's theme.) Frame the photo and present it to the subject.

189

Lend Your Energy

Offer to escort frail older persons to health care appointments, stores, or other needed services. Or you can help an elderly neighbor or acquaintance with home tasks, such as washing windows, shoveling snow, or painting. Bring friends along and make it a group project.

190

Make a Happier Home

If you have home repair or maintenance skills, repair and weatherize the home of a senior citizen in your community to ensure his or her safety and mobility. Set up routine help with homemaking, repairs, and maintenance through your Area Agency on Aging; use the Eldercare Locator at **eldercare.gov** or call 800-677-1116.

THOUGHTS THAT COUNT

People get jazzed when they can see the impact of their direct action. So when our volunteers see an elderly woman wheel herself out of her house and down a wheelchair ramp for the first time, they know that they have changed a life. When a low-income family with three generations living in four rooms sees volunteers adding another room, they know that their lives will be changed. Nothing beats the pride and satisfaction a team experiences from creating something that has lasting value. As we work toward a common goal, it binds us together and strips away differences. That's the joy of serving.

— Patty Johnson, president and CEO,
Rebuilding Together

191
Reengage Experience

Help a senior find a volunteer opportunity by contacting volunteer agencies in your area or visiting **seniorcorps .org** or **aoa.dhhs.gov** (click on Elders & Families, then Volunteer Opportunities). Older people can find validation in mentoring a child, tending animals in shelters, or visiting hospital patients — the options, like the rewards, are endless.

192
Compile a Picture of Health

Put together a health book in a three-ring binder for an older member of your family. Consult the person's doctors and medical records, then include lists of medications, their purpose, and dosages; dietary guidelines and recipes; doctors' names, numbers, and specialties; contact information for family, friends, and neighbors; blank pages for recording medical appointments and questions; and pockets for pamphlets and other papers. If possible, make copies for other family members.

193
Activate a Senior

Check with local churches or synagogues, senior and civic centers, parks, recreation associations, and even local shopping malls for exercise, wellness, or walking programs you can recommend to an older family member or friend.

194
Keep Fraud from Phoning

Seniors are a frequent target of telemarketing harassment and scams. Register a senior for the National Do Not Call registry; visit **donotcall.gov** or call 888-382-1222.

195

Acknowledge Solitary Spirits

At holidays, create and send cards with generic greetings to nursing homes and assisted-living centers. You can address cards to "All of my friends at [home or center name]" or call and ask for the names of residents.

196

Entertain at Home

Contact in-home senior service providers and ask if you can share your talent with their clients. Accompany them on their rounds and treat an older person to a performance, whether it's singing, playing a musical instrument, storytelling, dancing, theatrics, or doing magic tricks. Does your dog perform amazing feats? Ask if you can bring your pet, too.

197
Keep Friends Together

Assist an elder who has a pet: Offer to take the dog for a walk, clean out the cat's litter box, or shop for pet food and supplies. Provide transportation to, and support during, veterinary visits. Offer to feed a pet if an emergency arises.

198
Gain the Wisdom of the Ages

Take advantage of free advice from your wiser elders at **elderwisdomcircle.org**. Elder Wisdom Circle volunteer counselors share their accumulated experience and unique perspective with you via e-mail. You get a listening ear, and they affirm their valued role in society.

199

Protect the Valued and Vulnerable

Report any suspected incidents of elder abuse to nursing home directors or call your state's hotline to report abuse or neglect. Check the Social Service Organizations section of your Yellow Pages or find your state's number at **elderabusecenter.org** (click on Help for Elders and Families). Calls are confidential. For more information, visit the National Center on Elder Abuse at **elderabusecenter.org** or contact:

NATIONAL CENTER ON ELDER ABUSE
1201 15th Street NW, Suite 350
Washington, DC 20005-2800
202-898-2586
E-mail: ncea@nasua.org

CHAPTER TEN

United Nation

Not only is another world possible,
she is on her way. On a quiet day,
I can hear her breathing.

— Arundhati Roy

Even as the marketplace goes global and the world becomes more accessible, some things are still unique to American life. In particular, your rights as an American citizen reflect high ideals that are worth remembering — things we often take for granted until they are diminished. Regardless of your politics, our American identity is defined by the right to vote, the sacrifices of soldiers, a free press, and humane treatment. And if you disagree with the sometimes flawed practice of these principles, you also have the right to protest. Exercise your rights, if only because you *can*.

200

Hear from an Expert

Invite a speaker from Democracy Matters to bring topics such as "Money and Politics: Who Owns Democracy?" and "Elections as a Public Good" to your educational or civic group. Visit **democracymatters.org/SpeakersBureau/index.htm** or contact:

THE DEMOCRACY MATTERS INSTITUTE
2600 Johnny Cake Hill Road
Hamilton, NY 13346
315-824-4306

201

Supply Striving Students

Enlist your civic organization, faith community, or school in a collection drive for school supplies for Operation Iraqi Children. For a list of needed items, creative ideas, and a shipping address, visit **operationiraqichildren.org.**

202

Sign Up a Citizen

Encourage someone to vote and offer to go with him or her to register.

THOUGHTS THAT COUNT

A self-indulgent, "me-first" society will ultimately fail if we can't take care of one another. Here in America, we look up to and revere the individual: rock stars, sports heroes, politicians, and Hollywood celebrities. Meanwhile, right next to the White House, we have hundreds of homeless people. In many Third World places, a community's strength is judged not by the prosperity of the strongest or most famous person but by how well the weakest person in the community fares.

— Greg Mortenson, founder and executive director, Central Asia Institute

203

Collect Money for Morale

Have a simple fund-raiser — a yard sale, a bake sale, or a donation collection for your birthday or anniversary — and donate the proceeds to:

- The USO's Operation Phone Home program, which supplies American troops with prepaid phone cards to stay in touch with family and friends. Visit **usocares.org** for information.

- The USO's care package program, which sends personal supplies and snacks to deployed soldiers. Visit **usocares.org** for information.

- The "Voices from Home" program, which delivers free voice messages via e-mail from family members to troops. Visit **voicesfromhome.org** for details.

- "Gifts from the Homefront" gift certificates that troops can redeem at military base stores for merchandise such as health and beauty items, soft drinks, candy, snacks, prepaid calling cards, and music. See **aafes.com/docs/homefront.htm**.

Help Troops Befriend Kids

Donate basic goods, toys, or school supplies for American soldiers to give to children in nations recovering from war. Enter "help kids [name of nation]" into your Web search engine or try one of the following:

- Donate basic items to AdoptaPlatoon's Operation Crayon program; for a list of needs, e-mail operationcrayon@yahoo.com or write to:

  OPERATION CRAYON
  c/o AdoptaPlatoon
  PO Box 674
  Kingston, NH 03848

- Donate a Frisbee, a soccer ball, or school supplies to Spirit of America; find more information at **spiritofamerica.net** or e-mail staff@spiritofamerica.net.

205

Uncover the Truth

Learn about Freedom of Information laws and how they can help you access government documents (from the Environmental Protection Agency and the Occupational Safety and Health Administration, among others) that may reveal potential threats to the health, safety, and well-being of your community. The Reporters Committee for Freedom of the Press provides helpful instructions for invoking relevant state and federal laws to obtain government information. Visit **rcfp.org/foiact** or contact:

THE REPORTERS COMMITTEE
FOR FREEDOM OF THE PRESS
1815 N. Fort Myer Drive, Suite 900
Arlington, VA 22209
703-807-2100 or 800-336-4243
E-mail: rcfp@rcfp.org

Follow Campaign Funds

Reclaim government *by* the people, *for* the people. Sign up to receive *OUCH!*, a regular e-mail bulletin on how private money in politics hurts average citizens. *OUCH!* is published by Public Campaign, a nonpartisan nonprofit organization devoted to comprehensive campaign finance reform. Subscribe at **publicampaign.org/publications** or contact:

PUBLIC CAMPAIGN
1320 19th Street NW, Suite M-1
Washington, DC 20036
202-293-0222
E-mail: info@publiccampaign.org

207

Take Liberties

Order a set of six "Freedom is why we're here" magnets or a "You have the right NOT to remain silent" sticker from the American Civil Liberties Union at **aclu.org** (click on Store, then Logo Items). Or you can contact:

AMERICAN CIVIL LIBERTIES UNION
125 Broad Street, 18th Floor
New York, NY 10004
888-567-ACLU

208

Identify the Source

As U.S. citizens, we can only act upon what we know about. But our newspapers, television, and radio stations are rapidly being overtaken by a few corporate giants, limiting the points of view to which we're exposed. Find out who really owns the media in your town or city by entering your zip code into Public Integrity's Media Tracker at **publicintegrity.org/telecom.**

Demonstrate Your Character

Find out where to attend peaceful public demonstrations about social justice, nuclear disarmament, ending war, and other issues at **unitedforpeace.org** or **pax.protest.net.**

Claim Your Rights

December 15 is Bill of Rights Day. Do you know what your rights are? Download a copy at **billofrightsday.com,** print out the text at **billofrights.org,** or contact:

NATIONAL ARCHIVES AND RECORDS ADMINISTRATION
Research Support Branch, Room 406
700 Pennsylvania Avenue NW
Washington, DC 20408-0001
202-501-5235 or 866-325-7208

211

Experience War Stories

November 11 is Veterans Day. Embrace the stories of war veterans via letters, memoirs, audio recordings, and video interviews through the Library of Congress's "Experiencing War: Stories from the Veterans History Project" site at **loc.gov/folklife/vets/stories.** Ask relatives if they have photos or letters they can share from their own or others' wartime service. You'll learn more about our country and your relatives, become more aware of the realities of war, and honor the service of veterans.

212

Raise Voices with Votes

Help people without homes exercise their rights as U.S. citizens. Contact your local voter registration agency and ask how they're reaching Americans who are living in homeless shelters.

213
Don't Make Amends Lightly

Find out what it takes to amend the U.S. Constitution, and what amendments have been proposed and passed up to this point. Visit your local library or **usconstitution .net/constam.htm.**

214
Acknowledge a Price Paid

Help out for a day at a Veterans Administration hospital. Contact one near you and ask where your service might be needed.

THOUGHTS THAT COUNT

Consider the sustained effort that fought for the abolition of slavery and ultimately achieved desegregation; we are standing on the shoulders of generations of progress makers.

— Sarah Brady, chair,
The Brady Campaign to End Gun Violence

215

Advocate Student Exchange

Encourage your school to set up an exchange of letters or goods with a school in an area where U.S. troops are engaged. Enter "school exchange [name of nation]" in your Web search engine or try **spiritofamerica.net** (click on Get Involved); you can e-mail them at staff@spiritofamerica.net.

216

Find the Words

Understand the grief that survivors of fallen soldiers experience by reading first-person articles from the *TAPS Journal* (Tragedy Assistance Program for Survivors) at **taps.org/resources/articles**.

217
Know Your Lawmakers

Learn about issues that matter and the candidates' stands on them from the nonpartisan Project Vote Smart Website (**vote-smart.org**). You can check voting records of national and state legislators, find out their sources of campaign funding, and access key speeches and public statements.

218
Feast on Government Pork

Track your tax dollars. Browse *The Pig Book,* Citizens Against Government Waste's annual report on pork-barrel government spending. Visit **cagw.org** and click on Pig Book Summary or contact:

CITIZENS AGAINST GOVERNMENT WASTE
1301 Connecticut Avenue NW, Suite 400
Washington, DC 20036
202-467-5300

CHAPTER ELEVEN

Home Delivery

Nobody made a greater mistake
than he who did nothing because
he could do only a little.

— Sir Edmund Burke

When you take action on behalf of people without homes, your efforts can go well beyond providing four walls and a roof. Helping people who are experiencing homelessness can support their efforts to find employment, keep their children safe, and restore dignity to lives turned temporarily upside down. Recognize the humanity in the figure on the sidewalk, in the park, or in a line for blankets. He or she is probably someone's father, sister, former neighbor, or coworker. Lending a hand is easier than you might think. (To find a homeless shelter near you, check the Social Services listings in your Yellow Pages or enter "homeless shelter [your city or county]" into your favorite Web search engine.)

219

Put a Roof over Someone's Head

Spend a day with a hammer or paintbrush at a Habitat for Humanity home-building project. Contact your local chapter for information about upcoming "builds"; you'll find chapters listed at **habitat.org,** or you can contact:

HABITAT FOR HUMANITY INTERNATIONAL
121 Habitat Street
Americus, GA 31709
229-924-6935, ext. 2551 or 2552
E-mail: publicinfo@hfhi.org

THOUGHTS THAT COUNT

People ask where I find my motivation. The twenty-four million low-income homeowners in America spur me on. And while I wish there were more hours in a day, it still takes just a day to make a difference. Everyone is invited to join in — and that includes you.

— Patty Johnson, president and CEO, Rebuilding Together

220

Deliver the Comforts of Home

Upgrading your digs? Donate the furniture or household appliances you're replacing — in good condition — to a family transitioning into permanent housing. Go to **thenfba.org** to find a furniture bank near you, or contact:

THE NATIONAL FURNITURE BANK ASSOCIATION
538 Permalume Place
Atlanta, GA 30318
678-237-2000 or 800-781-8466

221

Work a Desk to Make a Home

If you can answer phones, type, file, or sort mail, you can help your local homeless shelter find funding and/or needed donations.

222

Ply Your Trade to Shelter Others

Whatever your job or hobby entails — catering, plumbing, accounting, management, carpentry, public relations, fund-raising, legal work, medical service, dentistry, writing, child care, or counseling — one day spent doing it at a local homeless shelter will prove its value.

223

Pitch In When "Homework" Has No Home

Help a young person at a homeless shelter with his or her homework.

224

Watch Your Language

Banish words like "bum," "transient," and even "the homeless" from your vocabulary, as these references strip people of their dignity. By referring to "people experiencing homelessness," you affirm their identities as human beings who are going through a difficult time in their lives.

225

Organize an Event at a Shelter

Contact a shelter and ask if you can bring board games, checkerboards, and chess sets for a preannounced Game Night — or gather musically inclined friends and offer to stage a performance.

226

Bring Play to a Shelter

Help your kids and their friends gather outgrown toys in good condition, and deliver them to your local homeless shelter in person — with the kids in tow. If you have no local shelter, you can mail the toys to a shelter listed at **hud.gov/homeless/hmlsagen.cfm.**

227

Help Make Homelessness Temporary

Donate work clothing, accessories, briefcases, and business supplies — in good condition — to a homeless shelter to help people who have job interviews. Offer to conduct mock interviews to give prospective applicants practice.

228

Prompt a Mail Campaign

Help shelter residents, staff members, and volunteers write letters to local and state lawmakers. Provide the shelter of your choice with paper, pens, addressed and stamped envelopes, and sample messages, which are available on many of the Websites mentioned in this chapter, such as **endhomelessness.org/pol/alert.**

229

Get the Public to Phone It In

Try "reverse panhandling." Compile small fact sheets (find source material at your library or on the Websites mentioned in this chapter) and work with your local shelter to organize residents and other volunteers to hand them out with quarters, asking passersby to call their legislators.

230
Stock a Reading Room

Find a shelter that would appreciate donations of books for adults and children. If you don't have a local shelter, choose one you can mail your books to at **hud.gov/ homeless/hmlsagen.cfm.** Send your own collection, and perhaps add variety by gathering books from friends as well.

231
Hand Off Your Recyclables

If you live in an area that gives refunds in exchange for recycled bottles, cans, and newspapers, either give bags of recyclables directly to a homeless person or, in a large city, leave sorted items in a location where a homeless individual can conveniently pick them up.

232

Create "Care Kits" for People on the Street

Put together kits with snacks, cups, utensils, soap, shampoo, toothpaste, toothbrushes, and cosmetics. During cold weather, add blankets, coats, hats, scarves, mittens, and socks. Contact a shelter or soup kitchen that distributes meals from a van and ask if they'll also hand out your kits.

THOUGHTS THAT COUNT

I am truly blessed to have the opportunity to make a difference every day. Rebuilding Together transforms houses, but it also transforms lives! While raising my four sons will always be my proudest accomplishment, my work with Rebuilding Together continues to give my life purpose, every day.

— Patty Johnson, president and CEO, Rebuilding Together

233

A Click a Day Keeps Homelessness at Bay

Make a free donation by visiting **endhomelessnessnow .org** and clicking on Donate Now! Your nearly effortless click prompts a site sponsor's donation, which supports a variety of organizations, named and described on the site, that aid people without homes.

234

Charge toward an Affordable Home

Many credit card issuers allow cardholders to either donate rewards-program points to charity or automatically donate a small percentage of their purchases to the charity you designate. For example, if you are an American Express Cardmember, you can donate your Membership Rewards points (which are then converted to cash) to Habitat for Humanity, Rebuilding Together, or other helping organizations.

235

Hold Politicians Accountable for Housing

Read about current government policy and congressional bills that affect low-income housing at **nlihc.org.** For more information:

NATIONAL LOW INCOME HOUSING COALITION
1012 Fourteenth Street NW, Suite 610
Washington, DC 20005
202-662-1530
E-mail: info@nlihc.org

236

Be a Shelter's Shuttle

Offer to drive children who live at a shelter to a special school event. Offer to drive their parents to a PTA meeting or other school program.

237

Plan for a Future with Adequate Housing

Read about the National Alliance to End Homelessness's "Ten Year Plan to End Homelessness" — an ambitious campaign to confront and overcome homelessness in America — at **naeh.org.** For more information, contact:

NATIONAL ALLIANCE TO END HOMELESSNESS
1518 K Street NW, Suite 206
Washington, DC 20005
202-638-1526
E-mail: naeh@naeh.org

238

Help a Shelter Resident Find a Job

A day at your computer can transform a life; become a virtual volunteer by going to **volunteermatch.org** and clicking on Virtual. For example, some shelters need volunteers to surf the Internet looking for entry-level job openings in different industries, then e-mail or fax their findings for posting on the shelter's job board.

239

Put Homelessness on Campus

Write a letter to your college alumni association or a local university encouraging them to participate in National Hunger and Homelessness Awareness Week. Help and materials are available from the National Student Campaign Against Hunger and Homelessness at **nscahh.org**, or you may contact them at:

THE NATIONAL STUDENT CAMPAIGN AGAINST
HUNGER AND HOMELESSNESS
233 North Pleasant Avenue
Amherst, MA 01002
413-253-6417 or 800-NO-HUNGR
E-mail: info@studentsagainsthunger.org

240

Hear About Homelessness

Invite people who are currently without homes, or who have been without homes in the past, to share their experiences as speakers at community meetings, schools, or church functions.

241

Craft a Warm Night's Sleep

If you're nimble with needles, knit or crochet a five-by-five-inch square and send it to End Homelessness Now's "Stitching Hope" campaign. They construct quilts and distribute them to people who can't find a bed at a shelter. If you're not so crafty, you can send yarn and knitting needles. The organization's regional contacts can be found at **endhomelessnessnow.org,** or you can contact:

END HOMELESSNESS NOW
STITCHING HOPE
PO Box 3374
Santa Clara, CA 95055
408-249-3516

242

Put Homelessness in the Headlines

Write a letter to the editor of your local newspaper advocating affordable housing. Visit the offices or Website of an organization that works to end homelessness for facts, figures, and guidance. Consult the Social Services listings in your Yellow Pages to find one, or log on to one of the Websites mentioned elsewhere in this chapter.

CHAPTER TWELVE

Creature Comfort

Just as the wave cannot exist for itself,
but is ever a part of the heaving surface
of the ocean, so must I never live my life
for itself, but always in the experience
which is going on around me.

— Albert Schweitzer

From the elephant on the African plain, to the grace of dolphins, to the dog or cat dozing in your living room, our fellow creatures are sources of both amazement and unconditional love. Yet many people are indifferent to the well-being of other creatures, and others abuse or kill them in the name of everything from profit to vengeance to sport. Animal cruelty should be a concern for all of us, because people who harm animals often enact violence against other human beings, too. Protecting natural habitat, providing caring homes, and generally respecting an animal's nature are compassionate acts. Here are some things you can do to show that you value our creature companions.

Treat a Monarch Like Royalty

Plant a butterfly garden. To learn how, go to your local library and ask the librarian to direct you to revelant resources. Or visit the Butterfly House on the Web at **butterflyhouse.org/gardening.html.**

244

Comfort a Furry Friend

Spend a day feeding, grooming, exercising, and talking to the residents of your local animal shelter.

Boost Farmers' Markets

Buy locally grown produce and animal products whenever possible. Supporting local, sustainable farming helps keep alive alternatives to industrial agribusiness, which often entails inhumane animal housing, transportation, and other practices.

246

Buy a Meal with Your Mouse

Help feed an abused, neglected, or abandoned dog or cat at no cost to you by clicking a single online button. Enter "click donations animals" into your favorite Web search engine or try the Animal Rescue Site (**animalrescuesite .com**). Your click generates a donation from site sponsors.

247

Speak Up for a Parrot

Learn about the plight of exotic birds who are kept as pets — and what you can do about it — from the Animal Protection Institute. Visit **api4animals.org/995.htm** or contact them at:

ANIMAL PROTECTION INSTITUTE
1122 S Street
Sacramento, CA 95814
916-447-3085

THOUGHTS THAT COUNT

Every person can make a difference for animals, every day, by making compassionate choices in the marketplace. The ten billion animals raised for food in the United States are kept in industrialized factory farms that typically do not provide them with room to turn around, or to stretch their limbs or wings. Millions of animals die in tests of common household products, such as detergents and toothpaste. And millions more — mink, foxes, chinchillas — are killed so their skins can be stitched into fur coats.

— Wayne Pacelle, president and CEO,
The Humane Society of the United States

248

Buy Coffee for a Song

Protect the habitat of migratory songbirds in Central and South America by buying shade-grown coffee, which encourages coffee farmers to preserve the tree canopy the birds require. Ask for it at Starbucks, Borders Books, and other cafés, or check the backs of packages for the words "shade grown" or an endorsement by the Rainforest Alliance or Smithsonian Migratory Bird Center.

249

Choose Human(e) Entertainment

Circus animals and other traveling animal acts endure radically different conditions than those nature intended. Avoid animal shows and public displays that include wild animals. Anytime an animal is caged, dressed in costume, trained to perform tricks, or exposed to stage lights, noise, crowds, and audience applause, it experiences severe stress — all for the sake of human entertainment. Patronize shows that only use human performers, such as Cirque du Soleil and Blue Men.

250

Let Fish Flourish

If you eat seafood, you can make choices that help sustain the oceans and overfished species by visiting the Monterey Bay Aquarium's Seafood Watch site (**mbayaq.org/cr/cr_seafoodwatch/sfw_regional.asp**). Read and/or download free wallet-sized cards that help you make mindful choices when dining out, or you can order cards by calling 831-647-6873.

251

Buck the Bronco

Choose to skip the rodeo. Rodeos often use electric prods, sharp sticks, bucking straps that provoke animals into violent motion, and other such devices. Calves can be injured and sometimes killed by roping practices — all in the name of "sport" or entertainment.

Give Declawers Paws

Download and make copies of the Friends of Animals brochure that explains why cats should not be declawed (**friendsofanimals.org/brochures/brochure.html**). Ask your local feline adoption center to hand them out with adopted animals, and share them with friends and family members who adopt cats. You can order copies through the mail by contacting:

FRIENDS OF ANIMALS
NATIONAL HEADQUARTERS
777 Post Road, Suite 205
Darien, CT 06820
203-656-1522
E-mail: info@friendsofanimals.org

253
Dismiss the Carriage

Horses and donkeys harnessed to haul tourist carriages are often malnourished and can be old, sick, or pregnant. Even if they are in good condition, these animals must carry very heavy loads for long periods of time, on road surfaces and in traffic that they were never meant to navigate. Choose another ride, or walk.

254
Look, Don't Touch

Choose not to swim with dolphins. These magnificent creatures thrive, without boundaries or obligation to humans, in the open ocean. They were never meant to live in tanks, pens, or other underwater enclosures to serve tourists or to perform for our entertainment.

255

Protest Big Cats as Pets

Find out what bills are currently being considered by legislators to keep people from acquiring lions and tigers as pets. Visit the Humane Society of the United States' "Bill Finder" page at **hsus.org/ace/11587**; scroll down and enter the key words "big cats" into the Bill Finder search box. After becoming informed, contact your representatives to voice your wishes. You can also request information from the Humane Society by contacting:

HUMANE SOCIETY OF THE UNITED STATES
2100 L Street NW
Washington, DC 20037
202-452-1100

Feed a Finch

Commercial bird feeders are available in most hardware and home improvement stores, but you can also make feeders out of plastic bottles or milk cartons and hang them in safe, out-of-the-way places. If you prefer to grow bird food, consider planting native wildflowers, shrubs, and sunflowers.

257

Give Animals Credit

Apply for the Defenders of Wildlife credit card at **defenders.org/shop**. For every one hundred dollars you charge, fifty cents will go toward Defenders' animal protection programs. For more information, contact:

DEFENDERS OF WILDLIFE
1130 17th Street NW
Washington, DC 20036
202-682-9400
E-mail: info@defenders.org

258

Spare a Guinea Pig

Choose cosmetic and household products that are not tested on laboratory animals. Look for the "leaping bunny" logo, which you can view at **leapingbunny.org,** of the Coalition for Consumer Information on Cosmetics (CCIC) or obtain a list of companies that have committed to this standard by calling 888-546-CCIC.

259

Eat Thoughtfully

Adopt a more humane diet by eating fewer animal products, even for a day or two a week, and choosing free-range, organic options when you do eat meat.

260

Say No to Fur

Make sure your coat's warmth comes from something other than fur. Also check hood, hat, scarf, and glove trim to avoid inadvertently flaunting fur. If you have a fur coat in your closet that you'd like to put to good use, donate it to the Humane Society of the United States; they'll turn it into bedding for injured and orphaned wildlife.

261

Prevent Snack Attacks

When you camp or hike, dispose of containers and food wrappings properly. Plastic wrap can suffocate animals, jars can get stuck on their heads, and plastic six-pack beverage rings can strangle. Rinse everything thoroughly, cut apart plastic rings and net bags, and throw everything into a tightly closed trash receptacle.

262

Keep Peace at Home

Reduce unnecessary conflict between neighborhood wildlife, people, and pets by taking the following measures: remove from your yard food and remnants, pet food, and scented candles that attract animals; maintain tightly lidded trash cans; collect ripe fruit from trees and the ground; and keep bird feeders in locations that predators can't reach.

THOUGHTS THAT COUNT

We can all help by eating lower on the food chain — fruits, vegetables, and grains — or by supporting producers whose free-range methods and other practices do not intensively confine the animals. In addition, we can purchase cruelty-free cosmetics and household products and reject garments made from animals' skins.

— Wayne Pacelle, president and CEO,
The Humane Society of the United States

263

Start Animal Awareness Early

Introduce a child to a Website that teaches animal sensitivity, such as Kind News Online (**kindnews.org**), an interactive site with fun animal-friendly activities. Ask your local elementary school administration to order and distribute the printed *Kind News* to its students monthly. You can also enter "kids help animals" into your favorite Web search engine, or try the ASPCA's **animaland.org** or the National Wildlife Federation's KidZone (**nwf.org/kids**).

264

Keep Kitty Inside

Keep your feline animal companions indoors; roaming cats are vulnerable to cars, poisons such as leaking antifreeze, enclosures that prevent escape, and people (often children) who take pleasure in taunting or even torturing them. If your pet does go outdoors, make sure it has an identification tag; lost or stolen pets can end up being put to death in a shelter or, worse, in research laboratories.

265

Take the Heat

Make your own information card about the dangers of leaving pets in parked cars, or order the packet entitled "Pet Welfare," which includes a reproducible version of this message, from American Humane (**americanhumane.org;** click on Publications, then Animals, then Care and Issues). You can leave the card on a windshield when you see a pet in a vehicle on a hot day. Call 866-242-1877 to order by credit card or contact:

AMERICAN HUMANE
63 Inverness Drive East
Englewood, CO 80112
800-227-4645

266

Help Critters with a Kit

Order the free Action Kit from the World Wildlife Fund. The kit highlights simple things you can do to help animals, and includes fun materials for the whole family, such as animal stickers and postcards, bookmarks, a fish fact card, and recipes for earth-friendly cleansers and insecticides. Visit **worldwildlife.org/act/signup.cfm** or contact:

WORLD WILDLIFE FUND
1250 24th Street NW
Washington, DC 20037
202-293-4800

CHAPTER THIRTEEN

Mind Matters

Never doubt that a small group of thoughtful,
committed citizens can change the world;
indeed, it's the only thing that ever has.

— Margaret Mead

At any age, learning is the key to growing as a human
being and creating a life of engagement and purpose.
The more you know, the greater the perspective you
bring to complex issues, and the greater the potential
for creative solutions. The love of learning takes root
in childhood and blossoms or withers by the grace of
many factors. You can steer a curious mind toward a
lifetime of educated exploration by taking the following actions.

267

Prepare Your Professional Successor

Serve as a "career day" speaker at a school. Contact your local schools to volunteer for a scheduled event; if there isn't one, suggest that they put one together.

268

Host Neighboring Scholars

If your home has a finished basement, recreation room, enclosed porch, or other spacious room, invite neighborhood kids over for a study and snack session.

THOUGHTS THAT COUNT

Taking a stand for justice, lifting one's voice above the din, requires faith in powers greater than ourselves. An awakening to God, perhaps, or trust in our inner voice — the god within.

— Peter Crosby, president and CEO, SeniorNet

269

Pass on Your PC

When you upgrade, donate your retiring computer to the Computers for Schools Program. They'll screen it for eligibility and quality; refurbish it through programs at correctional facilities, vocational centers, and community colleges; then place it with either a school you stipulate or another one in need. Visit **pcsforschools.org** or contact:

COMPUTERS FOR SCHOOLS PROGRAM
3642 N. Springfield Avenue
Chicago, IL 60618
800-939-6000

270

Pass On Your Knowledge

Volunteer to teach an informal one-time class at a continuing education center in your community. Subjects could be anything from how to use eBay, to effective time management, to starting a craft or catering business, or anything else you know about.

271

Ensure Education for All

Call your local schools and ask if they comply with the McKinney Act, the federal law that mandates educational services for homeless children. If the answer is "no," use the school's response to write a letter to Congress that outlines your local educators' challenges and concerns.

272

Visit the Doctor

Celebrate Read Across America Day annually on March 2, the birthday of Dr. Seuss. Read a Dr. Seuss classic to kids — or aloud to yourself (a guaranteed mood-lifter). If you do have an audience, don't stop at reading; discuss the books' messages about environmental conservation *(The Lorax)*, prejudice *(The Sneetches)*, commercialism *(How the Grinch Stole Christmas)*, and more. Visit **Seussville.com** for pure fun.

273
Network Nationally

Read about how communities around the country are working to integrate and strengthen their schools at Edutopia, a program of the George Lucas Educational Foundation. Visit **character.org/newsdialog/bboard;** you may get inspired to try something similar in your community.

274
Click Into Reading Resources

Introduce a child to Book Adventure (**bookadventure.org**), a free online reading motivation program sponsored by the Sylvan Learning Foundation for children in grades K–8. Children create their own book lists from more than 6,000 recommended titles, take multiple-choice quizzes on the books they've read, and earn points and prizes along the way.

275
Be Smart about Education

Find out from the National Education Association how you can be involved in your child's education. At **nea.org/parents,** you'll find tips on productive parent-teacher meetings, how to help kids with homework, and understanding standardized testing. Or you may contact:

NATIONAL EDUCATION ASSOCIATION
1201 16th Street NW
Washington, DC 20036-3290
202-833-4000

276
Take an Active Interest at Home

Read to your kids. Offer support and encouragement as you check their homework every night. Discuss their school day — *every* day.

277

Go Back to School

Meet teachers and visit their classrooms. Ask questions and listen thoughtfully. You don't have to have kids to acquaint yourself with local teachers; your tax dollars go toward hiring these professionals, and they are shaping young members of your community.

278

Enlist Community Aid

Ask your community's businesses, PTA, churches, and civic organizations to provide valuable services for schools. They can supply volunteers, sponsor evening or after-school tutoring programs, organize drives to collect school supplies for needy students, or raise funds for scholarships.

279
Endorse Commercial-Free Classrooms

Find out how much advertising your kids are exposed to in their learning environment. Do your schools have television in the classroom and, if so, are corporate sponsors' advertisements shown? Are cafeterias serving branded fast food? How many vending machines are on school grounds? If you're not happy about what you discover, let the school board know; you can arm yourself with information from Reclaim Democracy (**reclaim democracy.org/education/branded_schools.html**) and Arizona State University's Commercialism in Education Research Unit (**asu.edu/educ/epsl/CERU/CERU_Com munity_Corner.htm**).

280

Develop Student Character

Participate in a thought-provoking online conversation at the Character Education Partnership's bulletin boards (**character.org/newsdialog/bboard**). "Dedicated to developing moral character and civic virtue in our nation's youth as one means of creating a more compassionate and responsible society," the CEP invites discussion on such topics as partnerships between communities and schools, enacting character education initiatives, and education about diversity and character. For more information, contact:

THE CHARACTER EDUCATION PARTNERSHIP
1025 Connecticut Avenue NW, Suite 1011
Washington, DC 20036
800-988-8081

281

Subscribe to Higher Learning

Stay informed about current education issues by reading the National Education Association's online newsletter, *Thought and Action*. It highlights trends, legislation, resource material, and local, state, and national news in postsecondary education. Subscribe at **nea.org/he/tanda.html** or contact:

NATIONAL EDUCATION ASSOCIATION
1201 16th Street NW
Washington, DC 20036-3290
202-833-4000

282

Keep Classrooms Safe

Find out what your schools' safety and security measures are regarding weapons detection, bullying, assault, and related issues. If you aren't comfortable with what you learn, enter these terms into your favorite Web search engine to read about what other communities are doing.

283

Lobby for Learning Laws

Visit **nea.org/lac** to contact your legislators about pending legislation, sign up to become a cyber-lobbyist, and read updates on education-related laws. Or for related information, contact:

NATIONAL EDUCATION ASSOCIATION
1201 16th Street NW
Washington, DC 20036-3290
202-833-4000

284

Write All About It

Submit an article or letter to your local newspaper explaining why basic education, early college preparation, school revitalization, and teacher and staff training are essential to improving education. For more information, enter these terms into your favorite Web search engine or visit one of the Websites mentioned elsewhere in this chapter.

285

Invite Expert Input

Invite local educational leaders to speak to your civic or social group about the challenges they face and how you can help.

Stock a Learning Toolbox

Dig into a wealth of learning resources — tips, games, articles, and more, organized by grade level — at **scholastic.com/families,** or call 800-SCHOLASTIC for a product catalog offering award-winning educational books, toys, software, videos, and music.

287

Tackle Tough Topics

Supplement your child's education at home with the free lesson plans provided by Educators for Social Responsibility. You'll find a wealth of ways to explore current issues, such as war and discrimination, at **esrnational .org/sp/special.htm.** Or you can contact:

ESR NATIONAL CENTER
23 Garden Street
Cambridge, MA 02138
617-492-1764
E-mail: educators@esrnational.org

288

Greet Someone with Books

Support First Book, which supplies new books to low-income children, by buying your greeting cards from Heartfelt Charity Cards (**charitycards.com**). Ten percent of the proceeds go to First Book.

289

Buy Food for Thought

Support your schools with grocery shopping. Order from a wide array of products on the Website of Market Day (**marketday.com**), a food cooperative whose proceeds fund participating schools. Place your order in advance, then pick up your groceries at the participating school near you. Market Day dollars fund everything from computers and fine arts programs to field trips, books, and school equipment. If Market Day hasn't reached your community yet, pass the information on to your school leaders and suggest that they sign up.

THOUGHTS THAT COUNT

What excites me most is seeing a literate girl [in Afganistan] become a mother and instill the value of education in her children or, conversely, watching a literate girl teach her mother to read and write in the quiet evening by a dim lantern.

— Greg Mortenson, founder and executive director, Central Asia Institute

290
Make Cents with Global Education

Ask your local school, civic organization, or social group to launch a Pennies for Peace drive to support the non-profit Central Asia Institute (CAI), which builds schools for children in remote Pakistan and Afghanistan (where a penny buys a pencil). Young students collect pennies for a prescribed time period and donate the resulting collection to aid children abroad. For tips on implementation, visit **penniesforpeace.org** or **ikat.org** or contact:

PENNIES FOR PEACE
PO Box 7209
Bozeman, MT 59771
406-585-7841
E-mail: info@penniesforpeace.org

CHAPTER FOURTEEN

Food on the Table

It's not too late at all. You just do not
yet know what you are capable of.

— Mahatma Gandhi

Our minds must stretch to comprehend how people
can go hungry when our own cupboards overflow.
And yet there are probably people in your own community who choose between groceries and medicines
each month, who ration a can of beans among a
houseful of children, or who regularly visit the food
bank without their family's or friends' knowledge.
Circumstances in poor nations are much worse.
Pledge to take small steps to relieve this continuing
national and global tragedy.

291
Grow Your Own Solution to Hunger

An estimated 10,000 community gardens around the world give citizens a chance to cultivate their own food. If you hoe your own row, you can donate part of the harvest to your local food pantry or soup kitchen. Otherwise, pass along this do-it-yourself option to someone whose grocery budget is stretched thin. To find a community garden near you, contact the American Community Gardening Association (call 860-523-4276 or visit **communitygarden.org**) or your local USDA Cooperative Extension Service office. For more information:

AMERICAN COMMUNITY GARDEN ASSOCIATION
c/o Council on the Environment of New York City
51 Chambers Street, Suite 228
New York, NY 10007
877-ASK-ACGA

292

Collect Luscious Leftovers

Ask your favorite farmers' market, restaurant, grocery store, or large event organizer if you can pick one day to collect its excess quality food for delivery to your local food bank. To contribute on a slightly larger scale, you might also join a group gleaning event at a farm, in which volunteers collect crops that mechanical harvesters leave behind in the fields and donate them to food pantries. Contact FoodChain via **foodchain.org** or at 816-842-6006 or have your restaurants and grocers call 1-800-GLEAN-IT. For more information, visit **usda.gov/news/pubs/gleaning/content.htm** or write to:

USDA FOOD AND NUTRITION SERVICE
3101 Park Center Drive, Room 926
Alexandria, VA 22302

293

Bank on Decent Meals

Pick up and deliver, sort, repackage, or serve food at a food bank in your area. You can find one by looking under Social Service Organizations in your Yellow Pages or visiting Share Our Strength at **strength.org.** Kids can pitch in, too. For more information, contact:

SHARE OUR STRENGTH
1730 M Street NW, Suite 700
Washington, DC 20036
E-mail: info@strength.org

294

Help Kids Fight Hunger

Introduce a child to Heifer International's Read to Feed Website (**readtofeed.org**), where games, stories, resources, e-postcards, and other activities educate while entertaining.

295
Feel the Hunger

Fast for a day, or at least skip a meal, to begin to understand the impact of hunger relief efforts.

296
Test Your Hunger Quotient

Have your kids or young relatives take the Hunger Quiz at **kidscanmakeadifference.org.**

THOUGHTS THAT COUNT

We can eliminate hunger in America. We will develop the facilities; we will build the capacity of effective organizations. I like to think it will happen in my lifetime. I certainly think it will happen in my children's. We're building a foundation upon which others can work. And we know that whether we have the gratification of seeing our work finished or not, we're making a difference every day.

— Bill Shore, founder and executive director, Share Our Strength

---

297

Tell Congress to Feed the Children

Write to your state and federal representatives and ask them to put hunger on their agendas. Find information at **feedingchildrenbetter.org** or send an e-mail directly from **hungerfreeamerica.org** (click on Take Action). You can also influence congressional decisions by writing a letter to the editor of your local paper. Bread for the World's media staff can help; visit **bread.org** (click on How to Help, then Advocacy) or contact:

BREAD FOR THE WORLD
50 F Street NW, Suite 500
Washington, DC 20001
202-639-9400 or 800-82-BREAD

298

Bake a Batch of Hunger Relief

Team up with some friends and neighbors for the Great American Bake Sale; proceeds from your cookies will go to Share Our Strength, a national antihunger organization. Find out more at **greatamericanbakesale.org** or call 800-761-4227.

299
Make a Grocery List

Contact a food bank or food distribution agency and offer to develop a one-page wish list of the kinds of food the agency would prefer, as well as those it does not, such as cans vs. boxes and bags. Offer to distribute the list to local restaurants and grocery stores, and submit it to local media. If the organization already has such a list, offer to distribute it and suggest that they post it on their Website.

300
Go By the Book

Visit **fns.usda.gov/fsec/Resources.htm** to download a copy of *Together We Can!*, a handbook from the USDA Food and Nutrition Service that offers step-by-step plans for combating hunger in your community and elsewhere. Or you can contact:

USDA FOOD AND NUTRITION SERVICE
3101 Park Center Drive, Room 926
Alexandria, VA 22302

301

Promote Food as Art

Contact art, design, construction, or architecture companies in your area and suggest that they participate in the national CANStruction project (**canstruction.com**). Company teams of volunteers use cans of food to build clever sculptures for prizes and recognition, then donate the canned goods to a local food bank. If CANStruction isn't an option where you live, ask local companies to organize a similar promotional contest independently.

302

Brighten Up a Bag

Have a child help decorate grocery bags or boxes used at local food banks to identify special dietary needs (diabetic, low-salt, kosher, etc.). If there is a small, independent grocery store in your area, ask if children can draw and color pictures on its paper bags with "feed the hungry" messages.

303
Collect in Classrooms

Ask your child's school to sponsor a food drive or collect funds to donate to a hunger-relief program. Different grades, classrooms, or schools can compete to collect the most.

304
Invite Quick Food Collection

Ask everyone to bring a nonperishable food item to your next party, meeting, or social gathering. Donate the goods to your local food bank.

305
Launch a School "Team"

Find out if your local school participates in the USDA's Team Nutrition program, which ensures that students get healthy meals at school. Visit **fns.usda.gov/tn** for details or write to:

USDA FOOD AND NUTRITION SERVICE
3101 Park Center Drive, Room 926
Alexandria, VA 22302

306
Equip Food Gatherers

Donate harvesting tools that you no longer use to a community garden or gleaning project. Knives, hoes, pruning shears, long-handled shovels, gardening spades, spading forks, and rakes are all welcome, as are three-pronged hand cultivators, a hose, and watering cans.

 307
Grow Their Own

Ask your local school to start a fruit and vegetable garden, perhaps as part of class study. The project will help kids learn more about food sources, and it may contribute to their own lunch program — or they can donate the harvest to a local food bank or soup kitchen.

308
Pound It Out

Enlist the help of school officials and cafeteria workers to take one day (unannounced) to weigh the food kids leave on trays for disposal. Have them share the results with students and solicit suggestions from the kids for wasting less food.

309
Feed Your Expertise

Sign up at **frac.org** to receive the *FRAC News Digest,* a free weekly e-mail newsletter from the Food Research and Action Center. You'll be up to date on hunger, nutrition, and poverty issues in the United States. For more information:

FOOD RESEARCH AND ACTION CENTER
1875 Connecticut Avenue NW, Suite 540
Washington, DC 20009
202-986-2200

THOUGHTS THAT COUNT

In the United States, ending hunger really is a matter of creating the political will to do it. We certainly have the resources; we certainly have the money. One of the things that we don't have, frankly, is enough awareness. There are still not enough people demanding that we end hunger because there are not enough people who know that thirty-three million Americans are at risk for hunger or are using the services of food banks.

— Bill Shore, founder and executive director, Share Our Strength

310
Click Your Quick Support

Visit **thehungersite.org** and click the Give Free Food button; site sponsors make a donation to participating hunger relief organizations for every click.

311
Feed Poetic Souls

If your local bookstore or café hosts poetry readings, ask the management to dedicate a reading to the issue of hunger. Participants can read their own or others' poems related to hunger and poverty. Ask the staff to pass a hat for contributions to a local hunger-relief agency.

312
Get Results Online

Visit **results.org** and click on Take Action. Each month, the site posts a different action you can take that day to help alleviate hunger issues, including scripts for making phone calls to congressional representatives.

313
Deliver a Message

Ask local food-delivery services (pizza, Chinese food) to attach notices about food collections — either their own or another organization's — to their delivery orders.

CHAPTER FIFTEEN

Friends and Neighbors

Sometimes our light goes out but is blown
into flame by another human being.
Each of us owes deepest thanks to those
who have rekindled this light.

— Albert Schweitzer

Some of us are world-class neighbors and the kindest
of friends. Many of us intend to be, but we need an
occasional reminder. The rewards of strengthening
personal connections are always worth the effort.
Here are a few ideas, from the familiar to the more
uncommon, for reaching out within your own circle.

314
Express Yourself

Write to a friend you've lost touch with, someone you want to thank, your mom or dad, the teacher you'll never forget, or even someone in the news whose story touched you. Do it the old-fashioned way, with paper and pen.

315
Lend an Ear

Pledge to listen well for a day (to start). Eliminate distractions, look your companion in the eye, don't interrupt, and don't think about your response until the person speaking is finished. Ask questions of clarification rather than giving unsolicited advice or opinions.

316
Free Up a Parent

Offer to babysit for friends who desperately need a carefree night out.

317
Pinch-Hit for a Property

Keep an eye on an empty home in your neighborhood, whether the owner is a part-time resident or has passed away. (Grieving relatives may need time before they can attend to practical matters.) Mow the lawn, trim shrubs, collect deliveries, and see to minor maintenance.

THOUGHTS THAT COUNT

Young people today are volunteering more than any generation in history. Their service is equaled only by their tolerance, embracing their peers regardless of race, religion, gender, sexual orientation, disability, or cultural differences, all in the name of serving their communities together.

— Steven A. Culbertson, president and CEO, Youth Service America

318

Buy Some Time

Put a quarter in an expired parking meter at an occupied parking space.

319

Say Something Nice

Give out three compliments in a day, and direct at least one of them to someone you don't know. Admire the grocery clerk's memory for produce codes, the pizza deliverer's cold-weather endurance, the video store employee's movie recommendation.

320

Be the Best Medicine

Create and deliver a special "care kit" for a sick friend: soup, magazines, wooly socks, mentholated breathing strips, tissues with lotion for a sore nose.

321

Bring Home the Bacon

Offer to grocery-shop for a sick friend or housebound neighbor.

322
Clear Things Up

National Family Volunteer Day is held in November. Gather your clan, borrow some extra rakes or shovels, and offer to clear away neighbors' leaves or snow. When you're clearing snow and ice from your car, take an extra few minutes to do your neighbor's car without being asked.

323
Play Ann Landers

Know a friend who's down in the dumps? Drop by with popcorn and some great comedy videos.

324
Deliver a Dish

Never underestimate the power of a casserole or other homemade meal given to someone who is sick, infirm, grieving, or otherwise overwhelmed.

325
Reconnect with the Folks Next Door

Invite the neighbors on your block to an open house at your home, or organize an informal warm-weather block party.

326

Drive the Welcome Wagon

Are new neighbors moving in? Greet them with their first in-home meal, including plates and utensils so they don't have to unpack a kitchen box. (Take the dishes home with you so they don't have to wash them.) Deliver a list that includes your favorite dry cleaner, video store, bank, food delivery services, and other community resources.

327

Show That You Can Do

While you're moving your trash cans to or from the curb, haul your next-door neighbors' cans as well.

328

Make Driving Your Treat

On your way through the toll booth, pay for the car behind you.

329

Revive an Auto

Carry jumper cables in your car, and be prepared to use them when you spot someone in trouble.

THOUGHTS THAT COUNT

The problems facing our country and the world need young people's talents, skills, perspectives, and experiences *today*. We cannot simply flip a switch and expect youth to become engaged citizens when they become adults. Children as young as five years old can benefit from a service experience with their parents, siblings, teachers, and neighbors.

— Steven A. Culbertson, president and CEO, Youth Service America

330
Be a Neighborly 911

When new neighbors have school-age children, offer to be their "emergency contact" on school forms.

331
Help the Sick and Single

If your single friend lands in the hospital — especially if it happened unexpectedly — ask for a house key "to check on things," then clean the house and leave a favorite treat for your friend's return. Or, once your friend is recovering at home, deliver a meal, do yard work, or walk the restless dog. If you know a single parent whose children are sick, offer to run errands or deliver groceries while they are housebound.

332
Hit the Road

Cheer someone up with a "mystery ride." Make it spontaneous. Keep your destination secret; it could be your local ice cream shop, a picnic spot, or a town your friend has never visited. (If it matters, be sure to specify appropriate attire.) Try making the adventure something your friend wouldn't normally do.

333
Batten Down Hatches

If your neighbors aren't home when violent weather approaches, secure or bring in their trash cans and outdoor furniture.

334
Put It in Writing

Write down at least twenty-five things you like about
someone on individual slips of paper, then present them
in a small box or basket.

335
Acknowledge Pet Passings

Respond respectfully when a friend's or neighbor's pet
dies. Send a sympathy card, deliver a meal, or provide
information about pet grief counseling in your area. If
you know the person well enough, offer to accompany
your friend to a euthanization, or to contribute to or
attend a simple memorial service.

336

Practice Anonymous Altruism

Leave a Benevolent Planet "Tag Line" — a small card that extends your good wishes and invites the recipient to pass on the good will — at someone's door. Download a Tag Line for free at **benevolentplanet.com** (click on Tag Lines).

337

Make It Homemade

Revive a neighborly tradition. Pull out your favorite bread recipe, or find one at **breadrecipe.com,** and surprise a neighbor with a loaf warm from the oven.

CHAPTER SIXTEEN

Happier Holidays

What we sow is what we reap.
And when we choose actions that bring
happiness and success to others, the fruit
of our karma is happiness and success.

— Deepak Chopra

If your holiday spirit lags a little more each year — if dogs barking "Jingle Bells" join ringing cash registers to drown out the music of your season — vow to make changes this year. A simpler, more meaningful celebration can be yours, and it could give rise to new family traditions. Winter holidays aren't the only ones that merit reassessment; you can transform red-letter days year-round by adopting these simple suggestions.

338
Put a Bow on Gratitude

Offer to wrap holiday gifts for a struggling family through your area's Adopt-a-Family program. Contact your county or state department of social services for information.

339
Share the Wealth

If you find you have more baked goods, wreaths, or other gift items than you need around the holidays, take the extras to a community center, church, or homeless shelter.

340

Spread Some Light

Contact a hospice or nursing home and ask if you can help them decorate for holidays.

341

Look Past Picture-Perfect

Holiday celebrations often seem suited to conventional, fortunate lives: healthy, prospering families with all members together. Take a moment to think about those who may be in a different frame of mind: family, friends, or acquaintances who are hospitalized, mourning a loss, elderly and infirm, unemployed, alone, or far from family. Think of one thing you can do to brighten their spirits: visit, invite them to your holiday dinner, decorate their home, leave a package at their door, take them on a special outing.

342
Borrow from the Globe

Find out how other nations and cultures celebrate various holidays; visit your library or enter "holiday celebrations around world" into your favorite Web search engine. Adopt a tradition or two for your own observances.

343
Ask Santa for Support

If people are still shopping for that perfect gift for you, make their job easier and your own heart lighter. Ask them to support the organization of your choice with their time, effort, or a financial donation in your name. The organization's Website will tell them how.

THOUGHTS THAT COUNT

Some deep connection with the world around us — love, if you will — often makes social action not so much a choice as a burning spiritual need.

— Peter Crosby, president and CEO, SeniorNet

344
Make Holiday Headlines

If you've taken steps to put more meaning in your holiday this year, write a letter to the editor of your local newspaper and share your experience. Suggest that the paper do a story about it next year.

345
Celebrate Simply

Remind yourself that the best things in life are still free. For the December holidays, drive around to admire neighborhood light displays, take a winter walk, gather some friends to go caroling, watch holiday classics on TV, read seasonal tales around the fireplace.

346

Celebrate with Service

On major holidays, volunteer organizations sometimes need extra hands. Contact your area's Meals on Wheels program to see if they need delivery help. Call collection organizers and offer to sort and box goods. Or see if a Holiday Project group (**holiday-project.org**) is planning a visit to hospitals or nursing homes in your area. Visit **volunteermatch.com** and enter your zip code for other opportunities.

347

Think Out of the Box

December 26 is Boxing Day. This isn't about returning gifts, but rather it's based in a centuries-old British tradition of rewarding less fortunate people with gifts of durable goods or cash — presented in a box. Adapt the tradition: box something useful and deliver it to a homeless shelter, soup kitchen, community center, or church.

348

Give Greens a Second Life

If a real Christmas tree is part of your tradition, buy a live one you can replant after the holiday. If that's not an option and you get a cut tree, call your local trash pickup service, city government, or community management office to find out where you can have it recycled.

349

Think Before You Buy

When you buy holiday gifts, decorations, and supplies, remember conscious consumer principles, such as buying locally, choosing fair-trade goods, favoring environmentally friendly packaging, recycling or reusing, and buying things that last.

350

Spread the Donated Wealth

If businesses in your area all tend to collect toys or non-perishable foods during the holiday season, suggest to a business you frequent that they consider collecting other items. Holiday decorations, shoes and socks, firewood, books, and holiday music are all things that some people struggle to afford and would welcome at this time of year.

351

Leave No One Out

Send a holiday card — or several cards — with an all-purpose but genuine message to one or more residents of a homeless shelter. Or consider putting together a package of holiday cheer that all residents can enjoy.

352
Give Humanitarian Aid

Donate toward specific gifts with far-reaching rewards at **alternativegifts.org**, from a five-dollar home birth kit for an expectant mother in Haiti, to fourteen dollars for one person's water pasteurization in Tanzania, to forty dollars for an acre of sustainable cocoa farming in Belize. Alternative Gifts International is a collection of thirty-three sponsored relief and development projects in the United States and abroad that administer food, shelter, and environmental and social justice programs. Orders are taken online, and payment is accepted online or by phone, fax, or mail. For more information:

ALTERNATIVE GIFTS INTERNATIONAL
PO Box 3810
Wichita, KS 67201-3810
800-842-2243
E-mail: agi@altgifts.org

353
Buy Fairly from Artisans

Give a soapstone box, carved furniture, silver jewelry, or a traditional instrument made by craftspeople around the world who have been paid fair wages for their handiwork. Ten Thousand Villages has nonprofit stores in more than 180 U.S. locations in large cities and small towns. They also hold festival sales in additional locations throughout the year. Visit **tenthousandvillages.com** to find the one nearest you or contact:

TEN THOUSAND VILLAGES
704 Main Street
PO Box 500
Akron, PA 17501-0500
717-859-8100
E-mail: inquiry.us@tenthousandvillages.com

354
Give Back a Portion

Shop at an online charity mall, where up to 27 percent of your online purchases from hundreds of familiar merchants such as Barnes & Noble, Eddie Bauer, Sunglass Hut, Restoration Hardware, and Old Navy goes to support the cause of your choice. Enter "charity malls" into your favorite Web search engine or try **greatergood.com, igive.com,** or **buyforcharity.com.**

355
Purchase to Protect the Planet

Shop for eco-friendly gifts at **ecomall.com** (click on Gifts), where natural-fiber clothing, items from the Audubon Society, botanicals, and organic food baskets are just some of the intriguing choices.

356
Give from the Heart

Visit **newdream.org/holiday/giftideanew.html** for a long list of inexpensive, creative, eco-friendly gift ideas, from recorded audio or videotapes of family members' life stories, to calendars you make yourself. More great ways to invest your gifts with less glitz and more meaning can be found in the Big Love Gift Guide at **barkingowl.com/cc.**

357
Present It with Purpose

Use environmentally friendly wrappings: old fabrics, maps, sheet music, posters, newspapers, magazines, or even colorful junk mail, secured with organic cotton ribbons or hemp twine. Package gifts in reusable bags, or present them in new pillowcases, dishtowels, or baskets. Make your own wrapping paper by decorating paper bags with fallen leaves, twigs, and flowers from your yard, or purchase 100 percent postconsumer waste recycled wrapping paper.

358
Preserve Paper

Save money, trees, and your own sanity by sending an e-greeting instead of printed holiday cards. Truly beautiful animated greetings can be found at **hallmark.com, peacockcards.com,** or **care2.com.** If your recipient must have a tangible card, choose a nonanimated e-greeting and suggest, in your message, that they print it out on their color printer. Still feeling twinges of guilt? Follow up with a heartfelt New Year letter.

THOUGHTS THAT COUNT

A lot of young people have something that bothers or frustrates them, something they'd like to change, but they don't know how. At Do Something, we offer a five-step "Path to Change." The steps are See It, Believe It, Build It, Do It, Reflect.

— Nancy Lublin, founder, Dress for Success, and CEO, Do Something

---

359
Send Cards with a Message

If you must send printed cards, choose ones that benefit meaningful causes. Enter "holiday cards charities" into your favorite Web search engine or try Pasado's Safe Haven (**pasadosafehaven.org;** click on Gift Shop) to benefit this premier animal rescue organization; Studioworks (**studiowrkz.org**), whose cards are designed by at-risk students with creative talents in an after-school employment program; or Heartfelt Charity Cards (**charitycards.com**), which donates 10 percent of the purchase price to the participating charity of your choice.

360
Curb Your Assumptions

Remember that not everyone celebrates the same holidays you do, whether for religious reasons, out of personal beliefs, or due to circumstances such as parents' passing on (which can transform Mother's or Father's Day into a day of melancholy). Keep adoptive and foster students in mind when planning family-oriented programs. Plan group occasions and parties with sensitivity.

Mark a Year of Change

On New Year's Day, choose a single cause you would like to support for the year, whether it's youth programs, animal welfare, affordable housing, or antiviolence measures. Mark a day on your calendar for researching this issue online (click on What You Can Do buttons on Websites you visit) or in your local library to see what simple actions you can take throughout the year to make a difference.

Express Appreciation

If you celebrate Thanksgiving or another day of gratitude, display a box or bucket with blank slips of paper in your home and ask family and visitors to write what they are grateful for on the slips. (Make it available as early in the week or day as possible.) Read the slips before enjoying your holiday feast.

363

Play Easter Bunny

Whether or not you observe the religious holiday, take a stuffed bunny to your local hospital and ask them to give it to a special young patient.

364

Be a Secret Admirer

Buy a package of the silly, inexpensive valentines you exchanged in grade school. Mail them anonymously to family, friends, and random names from the phone book.

Rediscover Old-Fashioned Fun

Acquire an Activity Kit from The Legacy Project, a non-profit program whose aim is to strengthen the bonds between generations. With themes for the Holidays, Valentine's Day, Grandparents Day, and Mother's Day, the kits have crafts, games, homemade gift ideas, and more, all designed to bring families closer together. Download them for free at **legacyproject.org/activitykits.html** or order printed versions for a fee by calling the Communication Project at 800-772-7765.

Calendar of Monthly Events

For specific dates in any given year and simple ways to honor and celebrate these occasions, please visit **benevolentplanet.com** and click on Calendar.

January

National Mentoring Month
National Blood Donor Month
National Be On Purpose Month
International Quality of Life Month
New Year's Day/Universal Hour of Peace (noon)
National Bird Day
Universal Letter Writing Week
International Thank You Day
Humanitarian Day

Religious Freedom Day
Martin Luther King Day of Service
National Compliment Day

February

American Heart Month
National African American Heritage Month
National Bird Feeding Month
National Hot Breakfast Month
National Freedom Day
National Consumer Protection Week
Valentine's Day
Random Acts of Kindness Week
United Nations International Mother Language Day
Spay Day USA

March

American Red Cross Month
Arts Education Month
Deaf History Month
Help Someone See Month
Mental Retardation Awareness Month
Music in Our Schools Month
National Multiple Sclerosis Education and Awareness Month
Youth Art Month
Universal Human Beings Week
Read Across America
Peace Corps Day
Hug a GI Day
Girl Scout Day

Good Samaritan Involvement Day
National Animal Poison Prevention Week
Freedom of Information Day
National Common Courtesy Day
Companies That Care Day
International Earth Day
Great American Meat-Out
Anonymous Giving Week
International Day for Elimination of Racial Discrimination
World Day for Water
Arts Advocacy Days

April

National Prevention of Cruelty to Animals Month
Community Spirit Month
Keep America Beautiful Month
National Child Abuse Prevention Month
National Parkinson's Awareness Month
National Poetry Month
National Sexual Assault Awareness Month
World Habitat Awareness Month
Golden Rule Week
National Week of the Ocean
World Health Day
National Former Prisoners of War Recognition Day
Tax Day
National Youth Service Days
Consumer Awareness Week
Earth Day
National Volunteer Week

National Park Week
National Library Week
National TV Turn-Off Week
National Wildlife Week
Take Our Daughters and Sons to Work Day
Native American Heritage Day
Arbor Day
Spank-Out Day

May

**Melanoma/Skin Cancer Detection and Prevention
    Month**
National Bike Month
National Hepatitis Awareness Month
National Older Americans Month
Get Caught Reading Month
National Scholarship Month
Join Hands Day
Sibling Appreciation Day
Be Kind to Animals Week
National PTA Teachers Appreciation Week
National Nurses Day and Week
Mother Ocean Day
World Fair Trade Day
World Red Cross Day
Mother's Day
National Nursing Home Week
Peace Officer Memorial Day
National Waitstaff Day
National Missing Children's Day

National Senior Health and Fitness Day
International Jazz Day
Memorial Day and Prayer for Peace

June

Adopt a Shelter Cat Month
National Bless a Child Month
National Rivers Month
National Student Safety Month
Stand for Children Day
International Volunteers Week
National Hunger Awareness Day
National Trails Day
UN World Environment Day
Race Unity Day
Abused Women and Children's Awareness Day
Father's Day
World Refugee Day
National Forgiveness Week
Pick Up Some Litter Day
International Day in Support of Victims of Torture
Special Recreation for Disabled Day

July

Cell Phone Courtesy Month
National Purposeful Parenting Month
National Recreation and Parks Month
National Foreign Language Month
Canada Day

Air-Conditioning Appreciation Days
American Independence Day
World Population Day
Captive Nations Week
National Independent Retailers Week
Mutts Day

August

National Win with Civility Month
Friendship Day
National Kids Day
Sister's Day
National Night Out
UN International Day of the World's Indigenous People
UN International Youth Day
National Friendship Week

September

Children's Good Manners Month
Library Card Sign-Up Month
National Ovarian Cancer Awareness Month
Labor Day
National Assisted Living Week
UN International Literacy Day
One Day's Pay Event
Prostate Cancer Awareness Week
UN International Day for the Preservation of the Ozone
       Layer
Constitution Week/Citizenship Day

National Public Lands Day
Banned Books Week/Celebrating the Freedom to Read
Religious Freedom Week
International Coastal Cleanup Day
Deaf Awareness Week
National Dog Week
National Centenarians Day
World Tourism Day

October

Adopt a Shelter Dog Month
National Animal Safety and Protection Month
National Breast Cancer Awareness Month
National Communicate with Your Kid Month
National Crime Prevention Month
National Domestic Violence Awareness Month
UN International Day of Older Persons
World Vegetarian Day
National Custodial Workers Day
UN World Space Week
Mental Illness Awareness Week
Intergeneration Day
UN World Teachers Day
UN World Habitat Day
National School Lunch Week
National Children's Day
Thanksgiving (Canada)
World Food Day
UN International Day for the Eradication of Poverty
National Character Counts Week

National Make a Difference Day
National Day of Concern about Young People and
      Gun Violence
United Nations Day
Ramadan
National UNICEF Day

November

Adoption Month
AIDS Awareness Month
Alzheimer's Disease Month
American Indian Heritage Month
Diabetes Month
Epilepsy Awareness Month
Family Caregivers Month
Hospice Month
Lung Cancer Awareness Month
National Family Literacy Days
Veterans Day
World Kindness Day
America Recycles Day
UN International Day for Tolerance
National Geography Awareness Week
American Education Week
Children's Book Week
Great American Smoke-Out
UN Universal Children's Day
National Family Volunteer Day
National Family Week

UN International Day for Elimination of Violence
    against Women
Thanksgiving Day (United States)

December

**National Drunk and Drugged Driving Prevention
    Month**
Safe Toys and Gifts Month
Universal Human Rights Month
World AIDS Day
Rosa Parks Day
Tolerance Week
International Volunteer Day
National Pearl Harbor Remembrance Day
Human Rights Week
Bill of Rights Day
Hanukkah
World Peace Day
Christmas
Boxing Day
Kwanzaa
New Year's Eve

Acknowledgments

For his extraordinary creative talents and reliable good humor, I am deeply grateful to Bill Librizzi. For volunteering to be my chapter reviewers, I thank Bridget Anderson, Nancy Vittoria Bello, Dawn Bushey, Beth Carey, Diane Gray, Virginia LaForte, Zura Ledbetter, Laura Lively, Russ Mullen, Kim Murphy, Richard Sargent, and Michele Seiler. Thanks, too, to Guy Abernathey for making me smile. I'd also like to thank Elaine Faye and Ed Barberic, Ross Harris, and my brother Matt Jones for their remarkable generosity. Finally, I want to thank my Wednesday evening beach compatriots and the lively circle gathered regularly on the porch of At Melissa's Bed & Breakfast — including Melissa herself — for listening, responding, and affirming what is possible.

About the Author

Karen M. Jones is a creative strategist and social entrepreneur whose work comprises print media, Web content, creative products, and public presentations. Her most recent venture is Benevolent Planet, a source of simple strategies for socially conscious living.

As a professional writer and communications consultant for more than twenty years, she has had dozens of articles published in national and regional magazines, and has produced marketing materials for national membership organizations and international corporations. Karen lives with a cat named Jazz in Rehoboth Beach, Delaware.